It's Time to Walk on Water

Dan de Kock

PublishAmerica
Baltimore

ISBN: 978-1-4489-9742-8 (softcover)
ISBN: 978-1-4489-7297-5 (hardcover)
PUBLISHED BY PUBLISHAMERICA, LLLP
www.publishamerica.com
Baltimore

Printed in the United States of America

BIBLE QUOTATIONS

Table of Contents

FOREWORD

It is with great enthusiasm that I write this preface for "It's Time to Walk on Water." A walk of faith is always a necessity for anyone who is serious about being a dedicated Christ-follower. In a time when we have so many voices calling for our attention, our time and our hearts it is easy to lose sight of Christ and allow His voice to become distant. Since we are a part of the information age when information is expanding exponentially, it is tempting to live mainly by knowledge (man's understanding) and minimize wisdom (God's Word). Even though knowledge is very necessary, it is best to live by wisdom and revelation (that God still speaks to His people today). This book does a good job of helping you understand why this matters.

Dan de Kock has done a terrific job of step by step walking the reader of this book through a simple but complete process of what is involved in walking by faith. Since the Christian life is about walking by faith, there is nothing more important for us to focus on. Rarely have I read a book that cuts through the vast volume of verbiage that many books have and concisely gives you nugget after nugget, page after page. It is easy reading, yet thought provoking.

You cannot read this book without realizing that Dan is not writing about a theory he came up with or some new idea he had. He is writing out of a personal close walk of faith with God. There is a sincerity and personal honesty that he reveals from his own personal life journey that make the scripture and principles being taught come to life. This is more than just good information, it is truth lived out.

I now have known Dan long enough to say some things about him confidently. As he defines walking on water in this book—he walks on water! Dan lives to know Christ and make Him known. Even though Dan has walked with Christ now for many years and has a lot to share from that experience, I observe him to be an ongoing learner. Learners are the best teachers. Dan has come to the place of being an author not because he chose it as a career or many other seemingly conventional ways people come to write books, but because he has been walking on water. The only thing I could imagine that would make this book better is if Dan would make it an auditory book, reading it himself in his beautiful South African accent.

Rod Addison

Pastor, West Town Community Church

Evans, Georgia

PART 1

LAYING A FOUNDATION

As you therefore have received Christ Jesus the Lord, so walk in Him, rooted and built up in Him and established in the faith, as you have been taught, abounding in it with thanksgiving.

Colossians 2:6-7

CHAPTER 1
INTRODUCTION

Now in the fourth watch of the night Jesus went to them, walking on the sea. And when the disciples saw Him walking on the sea, they were troubled, saying, "It is a ghost!" And they cried out for fear. But immediately Jesus spoke to them, saying, "Be of good cheer! It is I; do not be afraid." And Peter answered Him and said, "Lord, if it is You, command me to come to You on the water." So He said, "Come." And when Peter had come down out of the boat, he walked on the water to go to Jesus. But when he saw that the wind was boisterous, he was afraid; and beginning to sink he cried out, saying, "Lord, save me!" And immediately Jesus stretched out His hand and caught him, and said to him, "O you of little faith, why did you doubt?"
Matthew 14:25-31

We are living in a season of turbulence and storms and change. God is shaking or allowing to be shaken, everything that can be shaken, and the Bible speaks accurately about this time in Hebrews 12:25-29. He alone is the unshakable One, and His kingdom alone is the unshakable kingdom. Everything that is not built on Christ and His Word is being or will be shaken.

Those who do not know Him are being given the opportunity to turn to the One who is unshakable, as the idols of man begin to collapse. We see the major economic storm that has hit this nation—and the world—and is affecting all who live in this land. Many have worshipped money and affluence rather than God, and the Lord is allowing this idol to be shaken to the core. He loves everyone, and wants to bring as many as will come into His kingdom before He returns. The shaking is bringing many to a realization that they can't make it on their own, and is bringing a new openness to faith in the Unshakable God who loves them.

The focus on material prosperity has also been detrimental to the Church in this nation, causing us to focus on things below rather than doing what the Bible says and focusing on things above. It has caused us to become lukewarm in our devotion to Christ, and to lose our way. We are called to seek first the kingdom of God and His righteousness, not material possessions and affluence, forgetting that if we do seek first Christ and His kingdom, He will provide what we need anyway. For those in the church who have lost their focus, the shaking is bringing a rude awakening to return to a first love relationship with Jesus, and to make the priorities of His kingdom their priorities!

While the time in which we live is challenging, it is also a time of great opportunity for those who have a first love for and genuine faith in Jesus as Lord. As believers we are being called to live a life of faith beyond what we are accustomed to, especially in the West. Our faith is being or will be stretched, and proved and refined. In the West many have fallen into the trap of thinking that having the right doctrine in our heads is sufficient. Nothing could be further from the truth. Christianity was never intended to be a mind only thing. It was always intended to be something that we lived out by faith in everyday life. This is going to become abundantly clear in the days we are living in, because if our faith is not as real in our hearts as it is in our minds, and if we don't live our faith in real life, it will prove inadequate. Faith grows more through one act of obedience to the Lord than through much doctrinal discussion. Good doctrine is essential, but if it does not affect our daily walk with the Lord, and if it does not issue in obedience to Him, we have missed what it is all about. It was never meant to give us swollen heads, but to result in humble adoration and faith and obedience to the One that we love.

The world needs to see people who LIVE BY FAITH! This is the challenge that this book attempts to address. When Peter began to walk on the water, His eyes were on Jesus and he was walking in faith on the word "come" that Jesus had spoken. **That one word had enough power to hold him up!** The Bible, in talking about Jesus in Hebrews 1:3, says that He upholds all things by the word of His power. He upholds the entire universe—all things—by the word of His power! Is He not able to uphold us in all things that we face? Now when Peter stopped focusing on Jesus and on His word "come" and started focusing on the boisterous wind that was churning up the sea beneath his feet, he began to sink. He was no longer walking in faith but in fear, doubt and unbelief. His faith had become unplugged from the Lord and His word, and was no longer operating. A lamp, unplugged from the wall cannot operate as it is disconnected from the power source. Jesus is the Author and Finisher of our faith, and when our eyes are on Him, and when we are focusing on what He says our faith operates wonderfully well. It is connected to the Power Source!

The Purpose of this Book

The Bible says, "The just shall live by faith" (Romans 1:17) and "For we walk by faith, not by sight." (2 Corinthians 5:7) We need to learn to walk on water over the storms that confront us in this time. We will face storms and situations and circumstances that will threaten to sink us, and we need to learn to walk through those storms by faith in the Lord and in His word to us. If we do not, we will be overwhelmed by the storms and will handle them no better than those who do not know Him. **The purpose of this book is to help take you into a realm of faith that you may never have lived in before, and to help you learn to live in that realm of faith as the normal way to live. We need to learn to live by faith as naturally as a fish lives in the sea.** Christians are designed to live by faith, but in the West many of us have been so sheltered by affluence and comfort and all the natural amenities available to us, that we live most of our lives without using our faith. That will not be adequate for the time that we have entered as much that we have depended on will be shaken. Many are already feeling the effects of uncertain gas prices and rising food prices, the mortgage crises, and the loss of jobs that is taking place as the economic uncertainty continues. We can respond to this in fear, anxiety and worry as the world around us responds, or we can rise to the challenge and grow in faith. There is no shortage in God's economy, and He is well able to "supply all your need according to His riches in glory by Christ Jesus" (Philippians 4:19). **God supplies our need in the visible world out of His kingdom in the eternal, unseen realm, and that provision is made available to us by faith.**

Most of us in this nation and other wealthy western nations have had a lifestyle of relative ease compared to the rest of the world. For many, Christianity has been reduced to going to church, which is good, but then living the rest of our lives by what we can see, touch and feel, in other words by the provision that we already have. I praise God for what I can see, but what happens when I can't see the provision or answers that I need? The theme of this book is to help you take your faith off the shelf, and to start using it in daily life as well as in crises and storms. **It is to help you learn to live as normally in the realm of faith as you have been living in the realm of the natural**—what you can see, taste, touch and feel. Then when what you can see fails, and when the natural things that you have relied upon prove to be unreliable, you will be able to walk on water by faith, and experience God meeting your needs! Nothing is too hard for Him. Nothing! He is the God who created the universe from nothing. If you are a believer, He is your Father and He cares for you. He is well able to take care of you in this time, well able! But He does ask you and me to trust Him. **It is time to learn to walk on water!**

Blessed is the man who trusts in the Lord,
And whose hope is the Lord.
For he shall be like a tree planted by the waters,
Which spreads out its roots by the river,
And will not fear when the heat comes;
But its leaf will be green,
And it will not be anxious in the year of drought,
Nor cease from yielding fruit.
Jeremiah 17:7-8

CHAPTER 2
RELATIONSHIP OR RELIGION

Do you have a personal relationship with Jesus Christ? No matter how religious you may be, no matter how often you go to church, and no matter how many good things you may have done, if you do not have a personal relationship with Jesus you are not saved. Even though Christianity is commonly presented as a religion, it is at the heart a relationship with God. If you know for certain that you are saved and that you have a real relationship with Jesus as your Savior and Lord, you don't need to read the rest of this chapter. **If you don't have a personal relationship with Jesus yet, this chapter is for you!**

Religion is basically man's way of trying to get right with God through good works, religious observances etc. Christianity is God making a way from His side for man to be right with Him. **Jesus is God's way. Religion is mans way.** How does a person enter into a relationship with God? Let us look at things from the beginning in Genesis.

God created man in His own image (Genesis 1:26-27). He did something that we would consider very risky. He gave man a free will, which meant he could choose to obey or disobey His Creator. God wanted people He could have fellowship and friendship with of their own free will. Most of us know that the first man, Adam and his wife Eve made the wrong choice. This was a choice with enormous consequences for the rest of mankind, because in rebelling against God, mankind became subject to Satan. God had given Adam control of the earth; he now lost that to the devil who then took control. Adam's disobedience broke his relationship with God, and so he was no longer able to have friendship and fellowship with Him. Instead, he now found himself dominated by an evil principality that not only hated God, but hated the creature that God had created. In place of being under the rule of a Benign God who loved him and had his best interests at heart, he now found himself under the rule of a malignant dictator who sought to destroy him.

The Creator stepped in to rescue his creation. He sent His Son Jesus to walk the earth as a perfect man who was in right relationship with God the Father. Just as Adam disobeyed God, Jesus lived in obedience to God, even to the extent of going to the cross and dying in our place. In the eternal scheme of things, Adams sin of disobedience was so serious that it incurred the death penalty. God could not just ignore it and say OK Adam, let's just forget about it. Adam's rebellion—sin—was like a deadly plague that spread to the rest of mankind. Sin separated man from God, who is the Source of all life, resulting in death. When Jesus died on the cross, a Divine exchange took place. Jesus, who was without sin, died in our place and paid the full penalty for all our sins. A person who receives Jesus and what He did for them, is credited by God with Jesus righteousness in place of their sin. That person receives a new nature, the nature of Jesus in place of their old sin nature, and is freely and fully forgiven for their sins. That person is also fully accepted by God, and restored into right relationship with Him. The obedience of Jesus restored to all who receive Him what Adam had lost.

Let us look at some Bible verses that will give us further understanding of God's plan of salvation, and lead us to the place of receiving that salvation which God provided for us by Jesus death on the cross.

"For all have sinned and fall short of the glory of God" (Romans 3:23). We were all born with a sin nature, inherited from Adam. Whether we consider ourselves good people, bad people or somewhere in between, not one of us has lived, or is able to live a perfect life. We may be able to do a good job of behaving well and looking good on the outside, but not one of us is able to change the sin nature in the inside of us and make it perfectly pure and like God's nature. Only one Man—Jesus—had a sinless nature, and could live as God originally intended. The first step in salvation is to take an honest look at ourselves and admit that we are sinners. This may be hard for our pride to swallow. But here is a sobering thought. Pride is probably the worst sin of them all. Pride is intimately linked to independence from God. It was Adam and Eve's desire to be independent from God—in a sense to be their own gods—that led to their disobedience.

"For the wages of sin *is* death, but the gift of God is eternal life in Christ Jesus our Lord" (Romans 6:23). Understand that without Jesus we are under a death sentence which is the consequence of our sin. This means that we are separated from God who is the Source of life, and that when we die we will experience eternal separation from God. The Bible makes it clear that without salvation we will wind up in hell, a place far worse than the worst place on the earth. This is a place that God designed for the devil and his angels, not for man. However, that is where we will spend eternity if we refuse God's provision of salvation through Jesus.

The Bible also says, **"For God so loved the world that He gave His only begotten Son, that whoever believes in Him should not perish but have everlasting life"** (John 3:16). God provided the way for you and me to be fully forgiven for our sins and to receive everlasting (eternal) life. The Bible makes another wonderful promise to you when you receive Jesus as your Savior and Lord. **"But as many as received Him, to them He gave the right to become children of God, to those who believe in His name: who were born, not of blood, nor of the will of the flesh, nor of the will of man, but of God"** (John 1:12-13). When you receive Him, you are born again spiritually with a new nature, the nature of Jesus, and become a child of God. Eternal life now begins for you, and your destination when you leave this life is Heaven!

Ask God to forgive you for all your sins. Ask Jesus to be your personal Savior and Lord. Thank Him for paying the price of all your sins, and for saving you from the consequences of sin. Thank Jesus out loud that He is now your Savior and Lord. Thank Father God that you are now one of His Children!

Chapter 3
THE FIRST PRIORITY

I am the vine, you are the branches. He who abides in Me, and I in him, bears much fruit; for without Me you can do nothing. If anyone does not abide in Me, he is cast out as a branch and is withered; and they gather them and throw them into the fire, and they are burned.

John 15:5-6

To step out of the boat of our comfort zones, and to start learning to walk on water requires faith. It requires faith in the Lord and faith in His word. This in turn requires a daily walk with the Lord, in which relationship with Him is our first priority. Anything less will not work. He must be number one in our lives in reality.

Once a person comes to Jesus and receives Him, there is nothing more important than maintaining our side of our relationship with Him. Abiding in Him needs to become and remain our first priority all the days of our lives. The alternative is given in the quotation above, and it is not an attractive one! To abide means to means to live, continue, remain, or dwell. This word, or a word that means the same thing, is repeated ten times in the first ten versus of John 15!

Consider a marriage. There is only one way for the fruit of children to be produced and that is the intimate relationship between man and wife. No amount of activity other than this will work. One of the saddest things is to see two people who start off their marriage truly in love with each other getting more and more busy. They both work as hard as they can to make as much money as possible to buy a big house in the best neighborhood, and buy the best cars. They strive to get promoted as fast as possible in their careers, and finally reach the place of achieving all this. And then for no apparent reason their marriage fails! The most valuable thing that they had was their precious relationship with each other, and that died from neglect. That is nothing sadder.

In the same way there is only one way for spiritual fruit to take place in our lives, and that is through an intimate relationship with the Lord. Many start the Christian life with a first love relationship with Jesus, and get sidetracked into other things. These other things may not be bad in themselves, but when they erode their relationship with Him, their spiritual life starts to dry up and their love for Jesus grows cold. After a while their Christian life becomes a dull, lifeless routine. It may look good on the outside, but the inside has dried up.

If we think of our lives as a wheel, then the hub of the wheel is our relationship with God. The other parts of our lives, marriage and family, work, ministry outside work, finances, hobbies and recreation, etc are the spokes of the wheel that radiate out from that central hub. When the Lord is the center of our life, it runs like a well balanced wheel. If anything else becomes central in our life, it runs like an out of balance wheel. An out of balance wheel will eventually fall apart. We live in a society that is falling apart because God is no longer central in it. As believers, no matter how fragmented our lives may have been when we came to Christ, if we make Him the center of our daily lives, they will progressively come into balance and order. There is nothing more important to our personal wellbeing, and to our witness to those around us, than our relationship with Him.

As a young believer, I wanted to be boots and all into Christian activity. I was overflowing with enthusiasm! However, I was putting the cart before the horse and my priorities were wrong. I was putting activity for the Lord before relationship with Him. Daniel 11:32 says, "the people who know their God shall be strong, and carry out *great exploits.*" I wanted to do great things for Him, but missed out the condition, the part about knowing Him. If you read John 15:1-17 in its entirety, it is clear that the fruit that comes out of our lives as Christians comes entirely out of our relationship with the Lord. The more intimate our relationship with Him becomes, the more fruitful our lives will become.

Sometimes we mistake frenetic activity in Christian service as fruitfulness. It may look impressive to us and to others, but unless it is a direct result of our relationship with the Lord, it amounts to nothing in His sight. Nothing! There is a restfulness that comes into our lives when we stop trying to be fruitful believers, and instead focus on abiding in Him. He promises to make us fruitful if we do abide in Him. That is His part, not ours.

God does not want us to do our works for Him, but He wants to do His works in and through us! We are not called to live a life of striving and straining, but of abiding in Him. If we do this we cannot avoid becoming more and more fruitful. His word promises it! It is so incredibly simple and restful that most of us miss it.

CHAPTER 4
THE VALUE OF OBEDIENCE

Obedience is the test of our love for God, and of our faith in Him.

The Test of Love

If you love Me, keep My commandments.
John 14:15
You are My friends if you do whatever I command you.
John 15:14

The test of our devotion to Him is obedience, the kind of obedience that is motivated by our love for Him, not out of a dry, impersonal obedience to the letter of the law. The Pharisees lived by the letter of the law, but for the most part had no relationship with God. They stood before Jesus the Living Word, and failed to recognize Him! We are not called to live by the letter of the law, but by a new and living way, the way of the Spirit. The Bible says, **"the letter kills, but the Spirit gives life"** (2 Corinthians 3:6). Those who live by the letter have missed what it is all about, as God wants a heart relationship with us. One of the tragic consequences of living by the letter is it kills relationships, not only our relationship with God, but also with others. There is no love in living by the letter of the law, only a dry slavish obedience that has no joy. True obedience is an adventure of faith as we walk with Him, and enjoy the adventure of life with Him. When we go His way instead of our own, and do what He wants us to, even when we would rather do something else, we demonstrate our love for Him. We find that He is not a slave driver, but a loving Lord who has our best interests at heart. When we choose to go His way, we find ourselves experiencing a joy and fulfillment that this world cannot give. **Jesus did not come to give us religion but life!**

We also experience a peace that comes because we are living in harmony with the One who created us and we are walking in the purposes that He created us to walk in. The road of "I did it my way" turns out to be a rocky road that gets worse the farther we go down it! When a cat is stroked the wrong way it is irritating to the cat. But if the cat turns round the opposite way, our stroking is soothing and appreciated. When we go our own way, life keeps stroking us the wrong way, but when we turn around and go His way, life starts to work for us. We are walking the way we were created to walk in!

The Test of Faith

By faith Abraham obeyed when he was called to go out to the place which he would receive as an inheritance. And he went out, not knowing where he was going.

Hebrews 11:8

Abraham demonstrated his faith by his obedience. Obedience is the action side of faith. The Bible says that "faith without works is dead" (James 2:20). I used to think that meant I had to run around doing good deeds to show that I had faith, until I realized that the works were works of simple obedience. If I had genuine faith in a certain area of my life, I would obey Him and do what He told me to do. **Our level of obedience is a good indicator of the level of our faith.** If we say we believe God, but don't do what He tells us to do, it shows that we don't really believe what He is saying. Our obedience is evidence of our faith. **The works that result from simple obedience are the good works that He has prepared for each of us to walk in.**

Some years ago the Lord gave me the following word: "Obedience is the doorway to My purposes and plans for your life. It is also a road that will take you farther and farther into My purposes and plans for your life." **We are called to live a lifestyle of faith, and true faith will result in a lifestyle of obedience.**

For many years I walked at the same level in my Christian life, and knew my way around in that level very well. I was like a student stuck in the third grade, and was unable to move up to the fourth grade. The time came when we started to attend a new church. I did not really know what to do in this church, as I liked teaching and there were no openings for teachers. The only place that was available for participation was early Morning Prayer at 6 am on Fridays. The thought crossed my mind that I should go to that, and I immediately put it out of my mind. Fridays were the last day of my workweek, and I was usually tired and did not want to have to get up earlier than usual when I felt beat. During the next three months the thought would cross my mind from time to time, but each time I would dismiss it.

Finally one day, I decided to give it a try. And when I went something wonderful began to happen. Firstly I really grew to love that prayer time with a few people to the extent that I looked forward to it as one of the highlights of the week. But not only that, the Lord began to move me into the next level in my Christian life. My simple act of finally obeying what the Lord had been trying to tell me for three months opened the way for Him to move me into the next level! I could have moved up three months earlier if I had obeyed Him sooner. **The lesson I had to learn before He could promote me was "JUST DO IT!"** When the Lord prompts us to do something, it is not for debate of discussion, but for obedience. That one act of simple obedience, to do what He said even though I did not want to do it, resulted in a blessing in my life beyond my expectations. The Christian life is meant to be very simple. Many of us just make it complicated. Since then, I resolved to simply obey the Lord first, and ask questions afterwards. Walking with Him in simple faith and obedience each day has become an exciting adventure. I don't do it perfectly but I am much quicker to "Just do it!

CHAPTER 5
A WONDERFUL PROMISE

If you abide in Me, and My words abide in you, you will ask what you desire, and it shall be done for you.
John 15:7

An integral part of abiding in Him is to have His words living in us. This is expanded in Joshua 1:8. "This Book of the Law shall not depart from your mouth, but you shall meditate in it day and night, that you may observe to do according to all that is written in it. For then you will make your way prosperous, and then you will have good success." For us who are in the New Testament, I believe we can take the Book of the Law to mean the Word of God—the whole Bible.

Having Jesus' words live in us starts with a regular diet of Bible reading, or if you don't like reading, listening to it being read. Jesus said, "*Man shall not live by bread alone, but by every word that proceeds from the mouth of God*" (Matthew 4:4). How strong would you be physically if you only had one meal a week? Many of us expect to be spiritually strong when the only meal we have in the Bible is once a week! We need a regular intake of the Bible to feed our spiritual person just as we need regular meals to feed our physical person. However, it does not stop there!

Jesus came to earth as the Word made flesh. For His words to live in us, they must be made flesh in us. They must change us on the inside to become more and more like Him! They must become so real to us that we live them out in our lives. It starts with reading or hearing the Bible. As we read or hear, there will be times when a particular verse or passage of Scripture comes alive to us. It makes sense and speaks to us. The next step is to meditate on that particular verse of passage. It is very helpful to have a journal, and this can be as simple as some sheets of paper in a three ring binder. It is good to write down what we get out of that piece of Scripture; what it means to us. As we ponder that Scripture it will get not only into our minds but also into our hearts. It will then start to affect what we say. Then the final step is where we start to do what that Scripture says. We obey what the Lord has said to us through it. Now that piece of Scripture is living in us! We have become a bit more like Jesus in that area of our lives.

The Holy Spirit is the One who helps us in this. He is our Helper, and our Teacher. He is the one who causes Scripture to come alive to us, and gives us revelation about what it means. **It is the combined action of the Spirit of God and the Word of God that changes us and makes us more like Jesus.** As we do what Joshua 1:8 says, it is God who changes us, not we ourselves. **But He does require our willing cooperation—our obedience.** As we live a lifestyle of daily fellowship with Him, and daily faith and obedience as best we know how, He will help us and guide us by His Spirit. He will reveal truth to us through His word, and He will pick us up each time we blow it. It is a learning experience, and I have learned more by trial and error than I like to admit. But God does not condemn us for making mistakes while we are learning, any more than we would condemn a child for making mistakes in learning to ride a bicycle. We would help them up each time and encourage them to have another try! That is how God is with us, except that He is a lot more patient than we are.

John 15:7 promises that if we do abide in Jesus, and let His words abide in us we can ask for what we desire and it will be done for us. If we are willing to satisfy the conditions, we will see results from our prayer lives that we did not think possible! **To the extent that do abide in Jesus, and to the extent that His words abide in us, we can ask what we**

desire and it will be granted. Clearly if we ask for something that does not line up with Jesus' words, it will not be granted. We also have to remember that everything we ask for will not happen immediately. Some things happen quickly, and others take time. The Bible says that we are to "imitate those who through faith and patience inherit the promises." (Hebrews 6:12)

God has a right time for things, and when He brings them to pass in His time that is the exact right time for them to happen. Just because something does not happen immediately, does not mean that God has not heard our request, or that He has said no. If we satisfy the conditions of John 15:7, and ask God something that is in our hearts to ask, I believe He will grant it because His word says He will, but it will happen in His time. Don't give up just because it does not happen right away. If we patiently continue to believe, it will happen down the track. And in the waiting God will do something good in our lives. We are interested in the results. God wants to answer our prayers, but He is also very interested in our character development—in our becoming more like Christ. On the way to receiving what we have asked for, God will do something in our lives to make us more like Jesus. If He does say no, it is because He is our loving Father and He has something better in mind. And when He answers our requests with the something better, we will be glad that He did!

We live in an instant society, where we have come to expect that everything must happen fast. If it does not, we get aggravated. Putting it another way, we live in a society that has little patience, and expects instant gratification. And when people can't have what they want, when they want it, they get miserable and complain. We have so much to be grateful for, and yet so many live as ungrateful complainers! I have discovered that when I get into a complaining attitude, God does not seem to hear what I say. It is as though He puts the receiver down and waits until I get out of that mode.

The Lord is looking for us to grow in maturity. One of the characteristics of a mature person is patience. A person who wants everything NOW is an immature person. We all begin as immature believers—there is no other way to begin. But God wants to take us on to maturity, and part of that is developing patience in us. The desire for instant gratification is one of the reasons for the high level of debt in our society, and as believers it is easy to get caught up in that way of living. However, God is patient and He is making us like himself. If we will wait for the Lord's right time and do what He tells us to do in the meantime, it will all work out. When we have to wait for something we grow a bit more patient, and we appreciate that something a whole lot more when it comes. In the process we become more grateful and appreciative of God's goodness, which is a much happier way to live. God knows what He is doing all the time, and He acts out of love for us and others all the time! **"He has made everything beautiful in its time"** (Ecclesiastes 3:11).

PART 2

THE ADVENTURE OF
WALKING ON WATER

Have I not commanded you? Be strong and of good courage; do not be afraid, nor be dismayed, for the Lord your God is with you wherever you go.
Joshua 1:9

CHAPTER 6
LEAVING THE COMFORT ZONE

And Jesus, walking by the Sea of Galilee, saw two brothers, Simon called Peter, and Andrew his brother, casting a net into the sea; for they were fishermen. Then He said to them, "Follow Me, and I will make you fishers of men."
Matthew 4:19-20
You therefore must endure hardship as a good soldier of Jesus Christ.
2 Timothy 2:3

One of the biggest hindrances to our faith is our comfort zone. We all have one. It is the place of the familiar and the known. We may not be pleased with that place, but we feel safe there. We know our way around in it, and we know where the boundaries are. As a teenager, my family lived in a seaside suburb. A swimming pool had been built out into the ocean, and at high tide the waves would break over the end of the pool and give one a taste of being in the open sea. It was a safe place for those who could not swim well; it had walls that were safe boundaries and it was a good place to learn to swim without danger. But there came a time when the taste was not enough, and I ventured out into the open sea. Now that was a whole different experience! It was a rocky beach so one could get injured on the rocks. Also there was sometimes a current that could pull one out, but it was exciting and adventurous. Once I had a taste of the open sea, and although I still enjoyed the pool, staying confined to it could not satisfy me. Greater adventure lay out in the open sea.

Our comfort zone is like that pool. We need a safe place in which to grow as new believers. But there comes a time when we cannot grow any more in the pool and we need to venture out beyond its confines. This is where many believers get stuck, and when that happens their faith ceases to grow, and the Christian life deteriorates into a dull boring routine. That is not the life, and life more abundantly that Jesus came to give us. Our faith cannot grow in our comfort zones. We need to be willing to venture outside them and to walk with Jesus in a much wider realm for our faith to grow, and for us to experience the abundant life that He promised

Consider Abraham who grew up in his native land and in his family environment. That was his comfort zone; that was familiar territory and that was fine while he was growing up. But there came a time for him to leave the known, for God had more, much more in mind for him!

Now the Lord had said to Abram:

"Get out of your country,
From your family
And from your father's house,
To a land that I will show you.
I will make you a great nation;
I will bless you
And make your name great;
And you shall be a blessing.
I will bless those who bless you,
I will curse him who curses you;
And in you all the families of the earth shall be blessed."
Genesis 12:1-3

Now Abram had a choice between staying where he was and living a life limited by his comfort zone, or stepping out into the unknown with God and fulfilling the destiny that God had for him. In chapter 3 we saw that "By faith Abraham obeyed when he was called to go out to a place which he would receive as an inheritance. And he went out, not knowing where he was going" (Hebrews 11:8). As a result of his faith and obedience he grew into his destiny and God changed his name from Abram to Abraham. His name was Abram in his comfort zone; it was expanded to Abraham, father of many nations, outside his comfort zone! He could have stayed where he was and lived out his life far below his destiny. He would have had a safe, predictable, unfulfilled and faithless life, but because he stepped out into the unknown with God, he grew into an amazing destiny.

God has More for Each of Us

Here we will introduce the theme that God has more for each of us than we realize. This will be discussed in more detail in a later chapter. It is sufficient to say here that the Lord gives us a taste of abundant life—of the more that He has for us—inside our comfort zones. He does this to show us that there is more, but we have to step out of our comfort zones to experience it. As long as we remain inside our comfort zones, our faith cannot grow beyond an immature level. When we venture outside our safe "box" with Him, our lives become an adventure of faith. **Just as Abraham had to leave the known and go out into the unknown with God to come into his destiny, we have to do the same to come into ours.**

It does not mean that everyone is called to leave his or her country or do what Abraham did, as God has a different plan for each of our lives, but we will have to leave something that we know and cling to, and launch out beyond what we know, clinging to Him. Launching out with God will require knowing what He is saying to us, as well as faith. However, although what He calls each of us to leave may be something entirely different, **the important thing is to hear Him and obey Him**. This is initially both a scary and exhilarating experience, but once one gets a taste of it, a life of safe, boring predictability in no longer satisfying.

We also discover that living outside our comfort zones with God is, in fact, a lot safer than clinging to our comfort zones. Everything that can be shaken is or will be shaken in this season, including our comfort zones.

But if we launch out with God, He is the unchanging, unshakable one; He will take care of us and He will provide for us. **There is a peace and security that can only be experienced in a faith walk with Him.**

CHAPTER 7
THE ADVENTURE BEGINS

Fear not, for I am with you;
Be not dismayed, for I am your God.
I will strengthen you,
Yes, I will help you,
I will uphold you with My righteous right hand.
Isaiah 41:10

When we step out of the comfort zone for the first time, it is normal to feel insecure. After all we are so accustomed to the known and familiar that it feels strange. Some years ago, my wife and I felt a persistent urging from the Lord to leave the church we were in. We had been there for about three years and felt at home there. We really did not want to leave, but as time went on the urging persisted. The Lord gave my wife a vision of a flower pot, where the plant had grown too big for the pot and the roots has burst through the sides. In looking back, I believe that the church we were in was like a good Middle School, but there comes a time when no matter how good the Middle School, it is time to move on to High School. For us to grow more in our faith and come into what the Lord had for us next, we had to leave what had become a comfort zone for us. The only problem was that we had no idea what to do next, absolutely none! Partly with reluctance and partly with a sense of adventure we left.

For a whole summer, we visited another church that was some distance away from home, and although we enjoyed it and grew there, we knew that it was too far away from where we lived for us to be able to do this in the long term. I kept asking the Lord what He had for us next, and the only answer He would give during that summer was "Trust in the Lord with all your heart, and lean not on your own understanding; in all your ways acknowledge Him, and He shall direct your paths"(Proverbs 3:5-6). I could not get past that Scripture! Finally, in the late summer, I came to the realization that the Lord wanted me to let go all my plans for my life. The hardest ones for me to let go were those that I wanted to do as a Christian serving Him. I thought they were really good plans! However, I realized that my own agenda was keeping us from what God had for us next. It was hard to do, but I quit all my plans, even my best ones. I prayed something like "Lord I have no plans; I just want to walk with You in your plans from now on." **The realization came that the Lord is the Plan Maker, and the simplest way to walk in His will is to walk daily with Him in simple faith and obedience.** The Christian life is meant to be simple. Not necessarily easy, but simple!

Looking back, that was part of what was involved in leaving my comfort zone behind. I had to get to the place where I was willing to follow Jesus into the unknown, as He had plans for my and our lives that we knew nothing about, and that in fact would turn out to be much better than our plans. **Our good plans can keep us from His best ones.** Hanging onto our own plans is a hindrance to coming into the full adventure of faith that He has for our lives. For me, it was both scary and wonderful to let God have the steering wheel of my life 100%. But when I did, a huge weight lifted off me. He was now in control of my life, not me anymore. A peace entered my soul that I had not walked in before. The control issue is deeply ingrained in most of us. We verbally and intellectually surrender the controls of our lives to God as believers, but the wonderful adventure of faith that God has for each of us cannot fully begin until we do surrender control in reality—in practice.

I began to learn to walk in a new level of faith and not sight, as I had no idea where I was going. I knew that the Lord knew, but I didn't. I was willing to go into the unknown with Him. Having spent seven years in College, and having been trained to figure everything out with my understanding, it took some getting used to, and I don't do it perfectly yet, but I have discovered that it is a great way to live. God is so much smarter than we are, and when the weight of figuring it all out is upon His shoulders, it is a much more restful way to live. The Bible says of Jesus, "For unto us a Child is born, unto us a Son is given; and the government will be upon His shoulder" (Isaiah 9:6a). **Simple obedience** replaced trying to work out the right course for my life at home, on the job, and in other ministry. As an old chorus says "Trust and obey, for there's no other way, to be happy in Jesus but to trust and obey." That is really true, and it really works!

This brings us back to the first priority. For Him to direct our paths, we need to spend regular unhurried time with Him, so we can become tuned in to what He is saying to us. We need His wisdom and His direction in our daily lives. He wants to lead us by His Spirit, but if our lives are so busy and so hurried that we have little or no time to cultivate our relationship with Him and hear His word, we will not be able to know His leading in our lives. If we are so busy that we do not have unhurried time for fellowship with Him we are too busy. We have become like Martha who was too busy with the practical things of life to spend time at Jesus feet listening to Him. There are certainly practical things to be done in this life, including our jobs, BUT they must not come first. Relationship with the Lord must have uncontested first place. In our culture it is harder to put the Lord first in our time than in any other area. We live in a very busy world that is traveling down the road at 90 miles an hour not knowing where it is going. **As believers we do need to know where we are going! And the only way to do that in this frenetic world is to give Him the first place in our time.** The first priority really is the first priority, and stepping out of the comfort zone will convince us like nothing else! We are in uncharted waters and we need Him to lead us on a daily basis.

Chapter 8
WALKING ON WATER 101

And Peter answered Him and said, "Lord, if it is You, command me to come to You on the water." So He said, "Come." And when Peter had come down out of the boat, he walked on the water to go to Jesus. But when he saw that the wind was boisterous, he was afraid; and beginning to sink he cried out, saying, "Lord save me!" And immediately Jesus stretched out His hand and caught him, and said to him, "O you of little faith, why did you doubt?"
Matthew 14: 28-31

Where is our focus? There has seldom been a time with as many negative and troubling things to focus on as there are now. Our focus will determine to a large extent whether we walk in victory or defeat, faith or fear in this time. The importance of focus is clearly demonstrated in the account of Peter walking on water. When Peter was focused on Jesus and His word "Come," he did something that defied the laws of Physics. He walked on water! Because of his focus, His faith was operating, and the power of the Lord and His word held him up. Amazing!

However, when his focus changed to looking at the waves beneath him and considering the boisterous wind which must have made the sea rough, he immediately started to sink. His faith had become unplugged and was no longer operating, and fear took over and sank him! This choice faces us today. Where is our focus?

In simple terms, walking on water is walking on the promises of God over the storms and through the winds of adversity that confront us, with our focus on Jesus, the Author and Finisher of our faith. We can do this by the power of God and His word operating through our faith. This is what Peter did when he began to walk on water. There may be a few in our day who actually walk on physical water in situations of extreme emergency, but this principle is applicable to all of us who have more conventional storms to face. When we focus on the storms and adversities that confront us, our faith becomes unplugged from the power of God, and we start to sink beneath the waves of our situations and circumstances. We can either be overcomers by the power of God operating through our faith, or we can be overcome by the storms that face us in these days. The choice is ours, and it is a choice which confronts us daily!

Faith and Presumption
I can do all things through Christ who strengthens me.
Philippians 4:13

I am the vine, you are the branches. He who abides in Me, and I in him, bears much fruit; for without Me you can do nothing.
John 15:5

The other thing that Peter did was to act on what Jesus had said. He did not act on his own initiative without Jesus word. He was smart enough to know that if he had stepped out of the boat without Jesus authorizing him to do it; he would have sunk like a stone! This leads us to the difference between faith and presumption.

Faith acts out of a dependant relationship on Jesus. Jesus Himself said that He did not act or speak independently, but acted and spoke out of a dependent relationship on Father God (John 5:19). If the Father did not authorize it, He did not do it!

Presumption acts and speaks independently from the Lord. It does not wait for the Lord's instructions, but jumps straight in and speaks or acts on its own authority. If we put the two verses quoted above together like two sides of a coin, we understand that we can do all things through Christ who strengthens us—all things that He wants us to do. We do not have the authority to go out and do whatever we want to do when we want to do it, even if it is a good idea! **If we are to walk on water, we need to learn to do what He wants us to do when He wants us to do it.** Both what we do, and when we do it, need to line up with His will. Then we will be able to do it in His enabling ability, and the responsibility of what happens will be His. If we do something on our own authority, we are stuck with doing it in our limited strength and wisdom and the results are our responsibility. Would you jump off a high diving board without checking to see if there is enough water in the pool? Choosing a course of action and then asking the Lord to bless what we want to do is the wrong way round. **If we do what He wants us to do, it will be blessed whether we ask Him to bless it or not!**

Living by Faith

God's word is always true; His promises are always true. God is a good God all the time, and He backs up His Word that contains His promises by His power. It is not our willpower that does the job, but His power! Learning to walk on water requires us to focus on Jesus, believe what He says, and act on it. Our actions demonstrate what we really believe. For those who presently have, or have had children growing up, you will have observed that if there is any difference between what you say and what you do, they will imitate what you do! **What you do shows what you really believe.** Children have an embarrassing way of keeping us honest.

Until we leave our comfort zones, there is very little to challenge our faith and make it grow. However, the moment we are willing to live beyond the boundaries of our comfort zones, our faith will be tested and it will be stretched and grow. When trials come will we run back to our comfort zones, or will we spend time finding out what God is saying in His Word and to our hearts, and then acting on what He says?

We all face different situations and circumstances that challenge our faith. These can get us down, or we can view them as opportunities to learn to walk on water. Our human reaction to a problem is to worry, and if it is a major problem, to walk around focusing on it until we sink beneath it. The first thing to learn to do—and it is not easy to do at first—is to hand the problem over to the Lord to solve for us. This requires taking time out to pray and talk to Him about it, and then handing it over to Him to take care of for us. God won't grab the problem out of our hands. If we want Him to take care of it, we have to give it to Him. The Bible instructs us to cast all our care upon Him for He cares for us (1 Peter 5:7). Sometimes I wake up during the night with a problem on my mind. I find that I cannot go back to sleep until I have committed it to Him and put it into His Hands. When I try to figure out a solution on my own, it just keeps me awake longer.

Does that mean that when we have handed a need or problem over to Him, there is nothing for us to do? Sometimes it means exactly that. Often there is something for us to do down the track, but only when He makes it clear what He wants us to do. The responsibility and control of handling the matter is now His, not ours, and this takes a big burden off us. Our only responsibility is to do what He tells us to do if and when He tells us to do it. Our part will never be the big part—that will always be His. In the process of the problem or need being dealt with, we need to keep our eyes on Him, and to hold onto whatever promise He gives us until it is solved. **That way we can get on with life, knowing that He is now in charge of the problem, and that the problem is no longer in charge of us!** We can walk on water over whatever is troubling us, in faith that God will take care of it in His perfect time. Nothing is too hard for Him!

Maintaining our Focus

Therefore we also, since we are surrounded by so great a cloud of witnesses, let us lay aside every weight, and the sin which so easily ensnares us, and let us run with endurance the race that is set before us, looking unto Jesus, the author and finisher of our faith, who for the joy that was set before Him endured the cross, despising the shame, and has sat down at the right hand of the throne of God.

Hebrews 12:1-2

There is nothing more important than maintaining our focus when it comes to walking on water. The simple acrostic below will help give you some basics of what it will take to learn to walk on water.

Focus on the Problem Solver, Jesus, not on the problem or storm.

Obey what the Lord tells you to do as best you can discern it. Don't do more than He tells you to, or you will start taking the problem back into your own hands, and get out of faith. If you make an honest mistake in hearing and obeying Him, it is all right. We all learn through mistakes, and the Lord will take care of the honest blunders that you and I make in learning to hear Him better.

Choose to believe His Word and His promises over and above whatever the circumstances or others may be saying. Jesus says, "Heaven and earth will pass away, but My words will by no means pass away" (Luke 21:33). His Word is the final word on any situation!

Understand that God reigns in that which concerns you, and He will work it out, solve it, and provide the need whatever it is. He may not work it out the way you want, but He will work out for your highest good. And He will work it out in His time.

Stay in faith until you see the answer, until you make it through the storm, until the need is met. Some things work out with amazing speed, some things take longer, and some things may take a very long time. We live in an instant society, and this can cause us to give up if we don't see immediate results. We need to "imitate those who through faith and patience inherit the promises" (Heb 6:12). In the meantime we can rest in the fact that God is taking care of what we have committed to Him, and that He will provide the need, solve the problem, carry you through the storm, whatever the situation. **Faith and patience will allow you to leave it all in His Hands, and free you up to enjoy and get on with the rest of life.**

GOD IS IN CONTROL!

Chapter 9
LIVING IN GOD'S PROVISION

But seek first the kingdom of God and His righteousness, and all these things shall be added to you.
Matthew 6:33

This is an amazing promise. It says that if we satisfy the conditions contained in this verse, God will provide all that we need. The context of this verse is our material and physical needs. In a time of much economic shaking and uncertainty, when prices are rising and our own personal economic future may not be as secure as we would like it to be, this is good news! I believe that this promise also extends to our other needs, as God is interested in the whole of our lives, spirit, soul and body. But what does it mean to seek first God's kingdom and His righteousness?

Let us look at the first part—seeking His kingdom first. Jesus is the King of the kingdom of God; so one thing it does mean is that our loyalty to Him must come before every other loyalty. It also means that relationship with Him and through Him with Father God must be central in our lives. The Lord is the center of the entire Universe, which He created, and we must make Him King and center of our universe—our lives. What seeking first His kingdom also means is that His kingdom must come before ours. In fact for this promise to really work, it requires laying down our own kingdom building completely, and being about the business of His kingdom instead. That is not the way of the world, which is very much involved with personal kingdom building. Jesus does not force anyone to lay down his or her own kingdoms—it is a voluntary thing.

When we live for self, the abundant life that we desire escapes us, but when we walk with Him and live for Him, we experience the abundant life that He promised, and a level of fulfillment beyond anything our own self-seeking could provide. **God made us and He knows what will fulfill us, and paradoxically when we stop chasing after self-fulfillment and start to put Him first, and to walk in His will for our lives instead of our own, we experience the very fulfillment that we were seeking!** When we put His interests first, He wonderfully takes care of ours. God is love and He wants the best for our lives. He is a loving Father and a wonderful Friend, not a harsh taskmaster. When we give Him our best—first place in our lives and affairs, He gives us His best for our lives!

"Then Jesus said to His disciples, 'If anyone desires to come after Me, let him deny himself, and take up his cross, and follow Me. For whoever desires to save his life will lose it, but whoever loses his life for My sake will find it'" (Matthew 16:24-25).

Let us look at the second part—seeking His righteousness. As those who have received Jesus as our Savior and Lord, He is our righteousness throughout all eternity. That never changes. However, God also wants to work the righteousness of Jesus into our lives so that we become righteous people in practice. This is a process that takes time as the ways of His kingdom progressively replace the ways of the kingdom of this world in us. However, at every point in this process of transformation, the righteousness of Jesus still clothes us and makes us 100% righteous before God.

God wants us to learn to live by the principles of His kingdom, which are different from the way that the kingdom of this world operates. **Entirely different!** For example, the world operates on fear and greed. We are to operate in faith that we have a loving heavenly Father who is taking care of us. The world operates on paying back a bad turn with a bad turn, whereas God's kingdom operates on forgiveness. We have been completely forgiven by God; we are required to walk in forgiveness towards others. The world operates on my money is mine and I will do whatever I want with it. The kingdom of God operates on giving the first part of our income to the Lord for His purposes, and trusting that He will supply all of our need out of His riches in glory in Christ Jesus. The world kingdom operates on fear, greed and lust. We are called to live in love, faith and purity.

The way we are to live is at direct odds with the kingdom of this world. Because it makes no sense to those who do not know the Lord, we will be misunderstood at times, even by unbelieving family and friends. Some may even ridicule us, but it is a small price to pay for learning to walk in God's ways. It is a test of how much we value learning God's ways. If we are willing to persevere, the Lord will teach us the principles of His kingdom by His Spirit and through His Word. It is a process of transformation that takes time, but as we continue walking with Him, His ways will be progressively established in our lives, and we will become more and more like Jesus. Faith will be required in this process, as there will be times when we do not understand God's ways of doing things. But as we start to act on our faith and obey, we start to understand His ways more and more, and we discover that they really work!

In summary, He simply requires us to be willing to do things His way, the way of His kingdom, instead of the old ways of the world that we used to live by. **God's promises are all true! And if we are willing to do what He says, we enter into the provision that He has promised.**

Is Anything too Hard for God?

In May 2007 the Lord began to speak to me about retiring. It started with a dream. One night I had one or those "Alice in Wonderland" dreams where nothing makes sense. In the middle of the dream a man stopped me on a flight of stairs and said "You will know when to quit," and I awoke sensing the Lord's Presence. Over the next few months events at work made it increasingly clear that it was time to retire. I was old enough but had a major problem—I could not afford to retire! We had a home equity loan and mortgage to pay off, and we were only just managing to make ends meet at present. A retirement income would be grossly insufficient. As time went on, it became even clearer that the Lord wanted me to retire. I had a choice between obeying the Lord and doing something that looked impossible for us financially or disobeying the Lord. Neither option felt good!

Finally, at the beginning of 2008 I plucked up the courage to inform my employer that I would retire, and that my last day of work would be in May. There were days when my faith was strong, and I believed that the Lord was going to provide although I had no idea how. On other days I had a sinking feeling in my stomach. Had I really heard the Lord? Should I really be doing this at a time when the economy was beginning to look as if a storm was on the horizon? Then things begin to happen, and it was as if the Lord opened the windows of Heaven. Several bonuses came in. Social Security kicked in, and a tax refund arrived. By sinking all of that into the home equity loan over the next few months, we were able to pay it off.

That still left the house mortgage. My daughter and son-in-law had written to us suggesting that we sell our home in North Carolina after I retired and come down to Georgia where we would be close to them and our five grandchildren. We liked the idea, but how? The housing market wasn't wonderful in our area in good times, let alone when the current market was as flat as a pancake. In the very unlikely event that our house did sell, it would take a long time and the amount we would receive after paying off the mortgage would be insufficient to buy another adequate house. We decided to shelve the move for several years. However, what is impossible for man is possible for God, as we were about to discover.

The week that I was due to retire, my wife was at the YMCA at the same time as a lady who had moved away from the area, but who now wanted to move back. She was looking for a house in our neighborhood. My wife on the spur of the moment said, "We have a house." The lady came round that same day and liked the house. That Friday, the day I stopped work, she put a deposit down on the house and the house was under contract! That was not the end of the story. Our house had been appraised several years before the slump, and she was willing to pay the full price before the slump.

Now we needed another house. Our daughter located a house for us in Georgia which we went down to investigate. It was a humble but nice home in a pleasant retirement community which had lakes, pretty scenery and various facilities to enjoy. It was only 15 minutes away from my daughter's home. We liked it, and because of the housing slump were able to negotiate a price significantly below the asking price. We moved down and took possession in early August. From the sale of our house in North Carolina, we were able to pay off the remainder of the mortgage on that home, pay all the moving expenses, and buy our new home for cash!

Is anything too hard for God?

CHAPTER 10
TRIALS

Faith

In this you greatly rejoice, though now for a little while, if need be, you have been grieved by various trials, that the genuineness of your faith, being much more precious than gold that perishes, though it is tested by fire, may be found to praise, honor, and glory at the revelation of Jesus Christ, whom having not seen you love.
1 Peter 1:6-8

Part of normal Christianity is that we experience trials. It is a part that we would gladly avoid, but both Old and New Testament saints experienced them. Trials test the genuineness of our faith, and also strengthen and purify it. **A trial free life is a growth free life!** God is more interested in our growth than in our comfort, while our tendency is to place our comfort before our growth. Although God allows trials, they do not generally come from Him, but from the enemy who is out to oppose us. The exception is when we walk in disobedience, or get off course. When Jonah went in the opposite direction from the one God called him to go in, God sent a storm that resulted in Jonah winding up in a whale. Not a good experience!

Many of the storms that we experience come because we are in a spiritual war against the forces of darkness that oppose us. Ephesians

6:10-12 gives us insight into this. "Finally, my brethren, be strong in the Lord and in the power of His might. Put on the whole armor of God, that you may be able to stand against the wiles of the devil. For we do not wrestle against flesh and blood, but against principalities, against powers, against the rulers of the darkness of this age, against spiritual *hosts* of wickedness in the heavenly *places*."

Trials also come to increase the quality of patience in our lives and to bring us into greater maturity. In fact Bible patience is not only the quality of being able to wait for something, but the quality of being able to endure and not give up.

Patience (Endurance)

My brethren, count it all joy when you fall into various trials, knowing that the testing of your faith produces patience. But let patience have its perfect work, that you may be perfect and complete, lacking nothing.
James 1:2-4

Some Bible versions use the word endurance instead of patience. Trials are instrumental in taking us from spiritual immaturity and raw recruits in the Lord's army, to making us mature saints and seasoned soldiers. We are instructed to have joy in the face of trials. On the face of it, that makes no sense! However, when we are able to see them as instruments in God's Hands to help shape us into the men and women that God wants us to be and to help prepare us for our destiny, we can have joy in the midst of them. In God's hands, they have a purpose—a good purpose! What the evil one throws at us for harm, God is able to turn around, and make work for our good. "And we know that all things work together for good to those who love God, to those who are the called according to *His* purpose" (Romans 8:28). God is able to make the good, the bad and the ugly work for our good! How does He do it? I don't know, but He is God, and nothing is too hard for Him!

And if the trial does happen as a result of our disobedience or of our making a mistake and getting off course, God will use it to get us back onto the path of His destiny for our lives. God is a good God who has our best interests at heart.

The Believer's Race

Therefore we also, since we are surrounded by so great a cloud of witnesses, let us lay aside every weight, and the sin which so easily ensnares us, and let us run with endurance the race that is set before us, looking unto Jesus, the author and finisher of our faith, who for the joy that was set before Him endured the cross, despising the shame, and has sat down at the right hand of the throne of God.

Hebrews 12:1-2

To run the race we are called to run certainly requires faith, but it also required endurance. Some translations use the word patience instead of endurance, but again Bible patience carries with it the quality of perseverance or endurance. We could describe it as patient endurance. If we try to run this race on faith alone, we will run it like a 100 yard dash and quit after a short time. But if we run it with both faith and patience, we will run with the mindset of a marathon runner, and have the staying power to keep on keeping on. It is one thing to begin the Christian race with great enthusiasm. Enthusiasm is good! But unless we develop the attitude of a long distance runner, we will not be able to complete it. **Trials are an important tool in developing that quality in us.**

God is with us and in us each step of the way, and He is the great Encourager in this race. We need to be tuned in to receive His encouragement directly and through others. We also need to tune out voices of discouragement, however they come. Discouragement is one of the evil ones weapons that he uses against us. God is an Encouraging God. The devil is a discouraging devil. **Who we listen to makes a big difference in the race!**

CHAPTER 11
WHAT WE SAY MATTERS

This Book of the Law shall not depart from your mouth, but you shall meditate in it day and night, that you may observe to do according to all that is written in it. For then you will make your way prosperous, and then you will have good success.
Joshua 1:8

What we say matters in our walk of faith. It is one of three things emphasized in the verse above that are necessary for our faith walk to succeed. A balanced life of faith includes saying what God says over and above the circumstances, needs, and storms that we face. It also includes meditating on what He says to get it into our hearts and minds, resulting in faith on the inside of us. And finally what we say and believe must issue in active obedience. When what we say and what we believe and what we do are in agreement with each other, our faith will be robust and work in practice! This kind or faith brings the promises of God into our lives and into the lives of others. This glorifies Jesus and is a witness of His love and power.

We Speak Life or Death
Death and life are in the power of the tongue, and those who love it will eat its fruit.
Proverbs 18:21

What we say has an important effect on us, and on others. The Bible says that "faith *comes* by hearing, and hearing by the word of God" (Romans 10:17). When we speak in fear and unbelief, we hear what we say and that undermines the faith on the inside of us. It can also undermine the faith of those who hear our words. We are sowing seeds of the wrong kind which produce fruit that we really don't want to eat! On the other hand when we speak in hope and faith, we encourage ourselves in the Lord, and we also encourage the faith of others. We are sowing seeds of life that will produce fruit that is good to eat. What kind or fruit do we want to produce?

For example, when I listen to too much negative news it leaves me feeling a bit depressed and anxious. Listening to someone speaking in faith and a positive attitude is faith building and lifts my spirit. God is a positive God. No matter what is going on, He still reigns, and His love and care still surround us who are His kids!

Faith is not Denial

In the world you will have tribulation; but be of good cheer, I have overcome the world.
John 16:33

One of the dilemmas that has puzzled me is that there sometimes seems to be a disconnect between people who are honest in admitting their problems and struggles, but find it hard to speak in faith, and those who speak in faith but find it hard to admit that they have struggles and difficulties. The truth is that in this life we will all have tribulation— storms, battles, and struggles. Jesus said that we would. The truth is also that He calls us to be people of faith in the midst of these things. Faith that only works when the sky is blue and the sun is shining is weak faith. Faith that pretends that we have no problems is superficial faith. We need the kind that will enable us to walk over the waves of the storms of life and into the teeth of the gale—overcoming faith! The promises that Jesus makes in Revelation are not to those who have no battles, but to those who overcome. Jesus overcame, and He wants us to become overcomers. How can we learn to be overcomers if we have nothing to overcome?

The norm for David in the psalms is thanksgiving and praise, but he is also a good example of someone who is able to be both honest about his struggles, and speak in faith. In Psalm 13, which is one example of this, he begins with his struggles.

To the Chief Musician. A Psalm of David.

How long, O Lord? Will You forget me forever?
How long will You hide Your face from me?
How long shall I take counsel in my soul,
Having sorrow in my heart daily?
How long will my enemy be exalted over me?
Psalms 13:1-2

He ends the psalm in faith:

But I have trusted in Your mercy;
My heart shall rejoice in Your salvation.
I will sing to the Lord,
Because He has dealt bountifully with me.
Psalms 13:5-6

He begins with refreshing honesty about his struggles. He ends with his focus on the Lord in faith and praise. When we deny that we have a need or a struggle we get no solution. God can't help us when we are in denial. It is like getting sick and going to the doctor. When the doctor asks what's wrong, we say "Nothing, we are fine." As a result we get no help! If we want help, we need to be honest with God and with ourselves about our situation. It is often helpful to have a few believers whom we know and trust and with whom we can share. They can help us to be honest, and can encourage us as we walk our way through the need, struggle or storm.

Having been honest, the next step is to turn our focus from the problem to the Problem Solver. We need to know what God says. The Bible contains many, many wonderful promises, and we need to find out what He says to us in it about our specific need or battle. We can then pray along the lines of His Word, knowing that His Word expresses His will. This will give us confidence that He will answer. "Now this is the confidence that we have in Him, that if we ask anything according to His will, He hears us. And if we know that He hears us, whatever we ask, we know that we have the petitions that we have asked of Him" (1 John 5:14-15).

Having prayed, we start saying what His Word says about the problem. This focuses us on God's answer and will strengthen our faith in the inside. **We are now walking on the water of our problem by faith!** Some needs will be met quickly; some storms will be over soon. Others may endure for some time, and require us to persevere in faith, positive confession of what God says, and obedient action until the need is met, or victory gained.

In Conclusion

Look also at ships: although they are so large and are driven by fierce winds, they are turned by a very small rudder wherever the pilot desires. Even so the tongue is a little member and boasts great things. See how great a forest a little fire kindles!
James 3:4-5

Our words matter more than most of us realize. God created the world by His Word. We create an atmosphere around us by our words. We can create an atmosphere of hope, faith and encouragement with our words. Or we can create the opposite—hopelessness, fear and discouragement. We can create an atmosphere conducive to peace, or one of strife. What kind of atmosphere do we want to live in and communicate to those around us?

There is a lot of bad stuff happening in the world today—Jesus said that there would be as the end of this age approaches. But what did He say we should do? He said, "Now when these things begin to happen, look up and lift up your heads, because your redemption draws near" (Luke 21:28). This is a precious promise that gives us hope in this time. **There** are many wonderful promises in the Bible that we can reflect on and that can be reflected in our speech for our personal encouragement, and for the encouragement of others. **Praise God!**

CHAPTER 12
THE POWER OF THANKFULNESS

Rejoice always, pray without ceasing, in everything give thanks; for this is the will of God in Christ Jesus for you.
1 Thessalonians 5:16-18

And we know that all things work together for good to those who love God, to those who are called according to His purpose.
Romans 8:28

A superficial examination of the first passage of Scripture may not make much sense. Why would we want to be thankful when things go wrong and we suffer loss or tragedy? It also says that this is God's will! However, if we dig into this more deeply, this passage does not tell us to thank God FOR everything, but IN everything. Also, this passage is not saying that it is God's will for bad things to happen to us, but rather that His will is for us to give thanks in the midst of whatever is going on in our lives. He is saying that no matter what is happening in our lives, whether good, bad or ugly; give thanks in the midst of it. This is a key to walking on the water in the face of adversity! It takes faith to do this, and this is where the second passage quoted above comes in. No matter what is happening in our lives, whether good, bad or ugly, God who is a good God ALL the time, is able to make those very things work for our good. In thanking God in the midst of what is happening we are saying "God we trust You to make this work for our good. We don't know how or when, but we believe that You will turn this round and that out the other end of this we will come out winners, not losers." This enables us to walk in victory over the waves and into the wind, knowing that the God, for whom nothing is impossible, will make it work for us in due time! That takes faith!

The alternative is to complain and be miserable about our situation and walk around feeling depressed. I don't know about you, but I have never found that complaining does a thing for me. It is as though God puts the receiver down and does not hear. But when we start to thank Him in the midst of whatever is troubling us, He starts to work on our behalf to turn things around, change things, or give us extra enabling to cope and make it through. When someone is going through a hard time and is asked how they are coping, we may get the response "As well as can be expected under the circumstances." The Lord does not want us to live under the circumstances but for the circumstances to be under us. **He wants to make us overcomers, not undercomers!** Giving thanks in the face of adversity or difficult circumstances puts us on the road to victory. In a real sense we are thanking the Lord for His solution in advance, even though we do not see it yet! And that is our faith in action.

One summer I was asked to teach a college level course in Physics. The Physics instructor had recently left the college and it turned out that I was the only full-time instructor who had the paper qualifications to teach this course. Although my major at college was Physics, my whole working life before starting teaching was in electronics. In fact I had been hired by the community college to teach electronics. I had taught a few classes in vocational level Physics, but this was a calculus based course. I had taken calculus at college in the days of slide rules before there were calculators, and had not used calculus since then. To say that my calculus was rusty was putting it mildly. I really, really, wanted to get out of this assignment, but the college was in a jam. Reluctantly I agreed to do it. The first day when I met the class I knew I was in trouble. These students were young and very bright and were doing their third college level course in calculus. They could have taught me, and I was supposed to be their teacher!

I struggled my way though the first couple of weeks, feeling a bit sorry for myself, and coping as best I could **under the circumstances**. Part way through the semester, I began to see that the Lord wanted me to thank and praise Him **in the circumstances**. I was more than willing to try something different! I started to thank Him and praise Him, not for the situation, but in the situation. The first thing that happened was that I started to feel better and more cheerful. The circumstances had not changed but I was starting to just feel better about it, even though I did not know how I was going to make it all the way to the end of the semester. The second thing that happened was that I found myself coping better with the teaching. The third thing that happened was that I had an experience of the Lord's enabling that was quite remarkable. One day, I had assigned the class to work on some problems that were quite difficult. If they got stuck, the instructors guide would help explain things, and I fully expected to use it. And sure enough they got stuck. And then something rather amazing happened. My mind shifted into a different gear. I clearly understood the subject matter with such clarity, that I could answer most or all of their questions without reference to the book. I simply understood both their questions and how to answer them without a struggle. I would like to say that all the problems classes were like that, but they weren't. But that unusual experience gave me the assurance that the Lord was helping me, and was quite capable of seeing me through the rest of the semester. And He did. At the end of the semester, the class took their calculus instructor and me out to lunch, and I really had the impression that they felt that they had had a worthwhile and good Physics class.

Giving God thanks in that situation changed something that could have been a very miserable experience into a rather wonderful experience of His ability to make things work for good. **When we give thanks in the midst of adverse circumstances, it is an expression of our faith which pleases God, and it gets us walking on water again.**

CHAPTER 13
DILIGENCE

The lazy man does not roast what he took in hunting,
But diligence is man's precious possession.
Proverbs 12:27

What Diligence is not
There are two things that diligence is not, the one is obvious and the other is less obvious. The obvious one is carelessness, and casualness; an indifferent attitude to things that are important. A careless attitude to these things will spell disaster in the days we are living in. We need to be diligent in those things that will make us and keep us spiritually fit and strong. We also need to be diligent in being good stewards of the physical bodies we have been given, if we want to be able to run the race that the Lord wants us to run. The Lord is not looking for couch potatoes, but soldiers in His army! I am sorry to be so blunt, but I have the same struggle not to become a couch potato as anyone else. I do not know when the Lord will return, but I firmly believe that we are in the season of His return, and that He wants us to redeem the time that we have and not waste it and squander it away. Each day is significant in His sight. Is it in ours?

The less obvious thing that diligence is not is a legalistic perfectionism that borders on obsession. This leads to an attitude of not doing anything unless we can do it perfectly, and this is stifling to creativity and the pioneering of new things. He who makes no mistakes makes nothing! There is a difference between giving something our best shot, and straining and striving to do it so perfectly that there is no room for mistakes. God does not want us to be strained, up tight people, always living on the edge of being stressed out. What kind of a witness is that to the unsaved? Why would they want to be like us if they are less stressed out than we are!?

True Diligence

The word diligence, or diligent, or diligently occurs more than 50 times in the Bible. The Lord clearly considers it is an important character trait. There are probably some areas in all of our lives where we are consistent and diligent, and others where we are not. A word that goes along with diligence is discipline, a word that has fallen largely out of favor these days. However, if we are to achieve anything of significance, discipline is a great ally. A person who wants to do well in any field must be consistent and disciplined. Natural talent can only take a person so far, and after that diligence in practicing that talent is essential if they are to excel. The same is true about our spiritual growth and development.

I believe that what the Lord is looking for is a wholehearted, willingness to do what He tells us to do, and persevere in doing it until it is done. In other words, He is looking for us to be **consistent and disciplined** in the things that matter to Him. We should give what we are doing our best shot as something done for Him. We should show up regularly for work, ministry etc, come rain or shine, whether we feel like it or not, unless we are really sick, or have to deal with a real emergency. But there is a balance between times of action and times to relax. God is a loving Father, who gives us breaks and times to relax and play. The Lord wants us to burn brightly for Him, not burn out!

Diligence will in fact benefit us greatly in every area of life. For example if we are diligent about living within a budget, we will be able to have freedom from the mountains of debt that a person without a budget will incur. Carelessness in any important area, will always lead to carrying an extra load of care down the road. Incidentally the same is true of procrastination. Procrastination now, will lead to needless pressure and hurry down the road.

Diligence and Reigning

The hand of diligent will rule,
But the lazy man will be put to forced labor.
Proverbs 12:24

Let us look at a few areas of life where we can reign by being diligent. This is by no means a complete list. Our physical health and well being is one of those areas. If we take the trouble to keep ourselves in shape through regular exercise, healthy eating etc, then our bodies will be able to do what we tell them to do. If we don't do this, our bodies will wind up telling us what we can and cannot do and our lives will become increasingly limited. Another example that has been already mentioned is our finances. If we are diligent in our budgeting and disciplined in our spending, we will be in control. If we are not, and indulge in uncontrolled spending, our finances spin out of control. Our debtors reign over us; they and not we rule our lives. Most of us have probably experienced this to some degree and it is not pleasant!

If we are diligent to spend time with our spouses, and appreciate them and go out of way for them, we will have a much stronger marriage. If we are negligent in our relationship with our spouse, our marriage is on shaky ground. When all the children grow up and leave home, will we still have a good marriage, or will it be an empty shell? After the Lord, our relationship with our spouse is the most valuable one that we have. It is worth investing time and love in it on a regular basis! In our jobs, if we are sloppy in arriving at work on time, and do the barest minimum of what is required of us, we will find that when the company we work for has to down size or lay off employees, we will be the first to go, and the last to be rehired. Now if we are diligent, we are more likely to be kept on in tough economic times. If we lose our jobs through no fault of our own, the Lord will certainly take care of us, for we have done what we can do, and He will do what He can do!

If we are spiritually out of shape—sporadic in spending time with the Lord, sporadic in feeding our spirits with the Bible, and sporadic in fellowship with other believers, then when a crisis in our lives arises, we will be spiritually unprepared to handle it. Just when we need to have strong faith, we will find our faith is weak. The crisis will reign over us, rather than us being able to cope with the crises. A casual approach to our relationship with the Lord will be nothing short of disastrous in the stormy times we are living in.

In summary, do we want to learn to reign in these and other areas of life, or do we want them to reign over us? Diligence is a big key in reigning in life. Now, I am not suggesting that we can do this in our own strength, but if we cooperate with the Lord in His making us diligent through our willing obedience, He will empower us by His Spirit to become diligent. He works in us daily "both to will and do for His good pleasure" (Philippians 2:13). Diligence needs to begin with our relationship with the Lord. **We need His power daily to become diligent and to be able to reign in life!**

Chapter 14
HEARING GOD'S VOICE

My sheep hear My voice, and I know them, and they follow Me.
John 10:27

This verse contains three characteristics of Jesus sheep. These are not the only characteristics, but they are important ones. Many are surprised when one says that one can hear from God. Even some Christians are surprised by this! However, Jesus said it, so it must be true. To hear His voice a person must have a real relationship with Him, which is expressed in the second part of this verse where He says He knows His sheep. The third part of this verse says that we follow Him, that is, we walk in fellowship with Him in simple faith and obedience to what He says to us.

The subject of hearing God's voice requires a book all by itself, and some excellent books have been written on this subject. In this chapter we will simply look at some of the basic ways that the Bible reveals about how the Lord communicates with us. The first thing to understand is that any relationship worth developing takes time, and what could be more important than developing our relationship with the Lord? There is no short cut to learning to consistently hear the Lord. It requires regular unhurried time with Him. The second thing to realize is that no matter how long we have been walking with the Lord, we can still make mistakes in hearing Him. Our batting average will certainly improve with time, but a humble awareness of our fallibility will help us to stay teachable and correctable in our walk with Him. Having a few good Christian friends that can tell us when we are going up a creek without a paddle is also big asset!

Now let's look at some of the ways of hearing His voice, starting with the two main ones.

The Bible

Your word is a lamp to my feet
And a light to my path.
Psalm 119:105

This is the first and foundational way of hearing His voice. Also it is **the reference** against which all other ways of hearing his voice must be judged. Anything that does not line up with the guidelines of Scripture is not His voice. The more familiar we are with the Bible, the more we will be able to hear what the Lord wants to communicate with us. I remember a senior saint telling me some years ago, "God sounds like the Bible." If we read the Bible regularly, there will be times when a verse or passage comes alive to us. That is God speaking to us personally through His Word! I encourage you to keep a journal and write down those passages, and what you get out of them. God wants a personal relationship with us, and He will speak to us personally through the Scriptures. Those who treat the Bible as a book of doctrine and no more have missed something very important! It certainly does contain the doctrines that we need, but it is much more than that! It is God speaking to us and revealing Himself to us through the pages of His Word. God is a personal God and He wants a personal relationship with each of us. The Pharisees who knew as much of the Word of God as had been written at that time, and who were experts in doctrine failed to recognize Jesus, the living Word of God. If they had had a personal relationship with God, they would surely have recognized Jesus when He walked among them.

We also hear God through the preaching, teaching and sharing of His word by other believers. The Lord has provided resources—people—in the Body of Christ to help us by sharing God's word with us through preaching and teaching. Ephesians 4:11-13 says, "And He Himself gave some *to be* apostles, some prophets, some evangelists, and some pastors and teachers, for the equipping of the saints for the work of ministry, for the edifying of the body of Christ, till we all come to the unity of the faith and of the knowledge of the Son of God, to a perfect man, to the measure of the stature of the fullness of Christ."

I believe He also wants us to have a few close friends that we can be honest with, and who can be honest with us in. We all have blind spots, and if we knew what they were they would not be blind spots! A few believers who know us well enough to speak the truth in love into our lives are a wonderful asset. The Bible says, "Faithful *are* the wounds of a friend" (Proverbs 27:6). We do not need flatterers, but friends who will encourage us AND who will be honest with us.

The leading of the Holy Spirit

For as many as are led by the Spirit of God, these are sons of God.
Romans 8:14

This is the second main way is hearing God's voice. The One who authored the Bible is the Holy Spirit and He lives in us who are believers. It is through the joint operation of the Word of God and the Spirit of God that we understand what the Lord is saying to us, and that we grow and mature as believers. A strong Christian is one who is full of the Word and full of the Spirit. Jesus exhorts us to let His words abide—live—in us (John 15:7) and the Bible exhorts us to be filled with the Spirit (Ephesians 5:18).

We are made up of three parts, spirit, soul, and body (1 Thessalonians 5:23). We were created to have fellowship with God who is spirit, but when Adam fell his spirit was no longer alive, so he could no longer hear God with his spirit. He had to rely on his mind, will and emotions (his soul) to lead him. So man began to live out of his soul realm, and unsaved man operates that way to this day. We who are born again are spiritually alive, and have the capacity to hear the Holy Spirit and be led by Him. However, we still tend to operate largely out of the soul realm because that is how we used to operate.

In the natural, we tend to be led by our intellects, our emotions or our wills. Men are most likely to rely on their intellects and woman by their feelings which keep our marriages interesting! Very strong willed people tend to be led by their wills. However, these are all operations of the soul realm. **If we are to mature as believers and grow from spiritual childhood into sons, we need to learn to be led by the Spirit.** Incidentally men and woman are both sons spiritually (Galatians 3:26-28). Our minds, wills and emotions are extremely valuable, given to us by God, but they have to be submitted to our spirits if we are to have fellowship with and be led by the Lord. It is a learning experience that takes practice, and God is a loving and patient Father in helping us to learn. The more we walk in the Spirit, the more our minds, wills and emotions will be released to operate the way God designed them to operate.

The main hindrance that faced me in learning to be led by the Spirit was my tendency to always rely on my logical thinking, and to be led by that even when the Lord was directing me a different way. If I felt an inner urging to do something or not do something I would rationalize it away if I could see no immediate reason to do it. I successfully missed the Lord a number of times before starting to learn. There is nothing wrong with having a logical mind—it as an asset. But it must not override what God is saying, for He is much smarter than we are. He sees the whole picture in any decision we are faced with and knows the future. **When our reasoning tells us something different from how He is leading us, it is smart to do what He says!** How does the Holy Spirit lead us? I do not know all the answers, but will share some ways that I have learned.

One way He directs us is through a persistent inner urging or thought. How do we know the difference between just our own feelings and thoughts and His leading? Practice! Clearly, He won't tell us to do anything that goes against the Bible. Apart from that, it is learning experience requiring plenty of practice. We would not condemn a child making mistakes learning to tie their shoelaces, or learning to ride a bicycle, but would encourage them and help them to learn through their mistakes. In the same way the Lord does not condemn us for our blunders in learning, but encourages us and helps us to keep trying until we get it.

There in no way to learn something new without making mistakes. I have never met a person yet who learned to ride a bicycle without unsuccessful attempts to start with! I crashed into a thorny hedge in our yard a number of times before getting the hang of it. A child that is not allowed to make mistakes cannot learn, nor can we learn spiritually unless we are willing to make mistakes. The Lord is wonderfully kind and patient with us in helping us and encouraging us as we learn.

How else does the Holy Spirit lead us? One way is through wisdom. There are times when we do not know what to do, or how to handle a specific situation, and we suddenly know what to do. The Holy Spirit drops the solution into our minds. At other times, as we read the Bible, a verse or passage will speak to our situation. That is the Holy Spirit speaking to us through His Word. In times of Christian fellowship, He will speak to us through each other as we share together.

Another way He leads us is by peace. Isaiah 55:12 says, "For you shall go out with joy, and be led out with peace." When we are walking in the will of God for our lives, there is an inner peace that we experience. When something disturbs that peace, it is a warning that something is wrong. When making a decision, I have learned to wait for that inner confirming peace. We may make a decision that looks right to us and to others, that makes sense, but if that peace is not there it is wise to wait up and seek the Lord further. It is so easy to decide something because it looks good on the surface, but the Lord sees below the surface and knows what is really good for us and our households. The Holy Spirit is also the Spirit of Truth, and He will witness to the truth. As a young believer, I was listening to a talk given by a well-known Christian speaker. At one point he said something that just did not ring true to me on the inside. I did not know my Bible well enough at that time to know why it did not feel right, but when I got home I dug through the Bible, and sure enough, what had been said was not right. The Holy Spirit had disturbed my peace on the inside to let me know that what had been said was not true. This is not a criticism of the speaker—the rest of the message was good and we all make mistakes—but the Lord was teaching me to listen to His voice and to give that priority over every other voice. Praise Him! There is a beautiful verse that says, "Her ways are ways of pleasantness, and all her paths are peace" (Proverbs 3:17). This is speaking about wisdom. When we walk in the leading of the Holy Spirit we are walking in wisdom and His ways are pleasant ways and ways of peace. **In the world as it is today, which has much knowledge and little wisdom, and very little peace, we need to walk in His ways as never before.**

The operation of the gifts of the Spirit
For the manifestation of the Spirit is given to each one for the profit of all.
1 Corinthians 12:7

There is a lot that can be said about them and a very brief introduction is given here. 1 Corinthians 12:8-10 outlines the specific gifts of the Spirit that operated in the early church. These are still available to the church today, and can operate in individual or corporate ministry. They can operate in the church and in the market place. Let us look at each of the gifts that are specifically related to hearing God's voice. The purpose of the **gift of prophecy** is given in 1 Corinthians 14:3. "But he who prophesies speaks edification and exhortation and comfort to men." The person who prophesies hears—discerns, understands—something that God is saying to a person or congregation and expresses it. Its purpose is entirely positive as outlined in the verse above. The gift of prophesy is available to every believer, but that does not mean that the prophetic calling is available to every believer. For example, not every believer is called to be a pastor, or teacher or evangelist etc. But whatever our individual calling may be, it has the potential to be enriched by the gift of prophecy. The gift of prophecy can be a powerful source of encouragement to an individual believer or congregation. The **gift of tongues with interpretation** can essentially achieve the same purpose.

The gift of a **word of wisdom** expresses revelation by God concerning a situation, problem or circumstance, giving helpful insight from the Lord as to what to do concerning the matter. The **word of knowledge** is information given supernaturally by God. For example a person may be shown a specific illness in someone in a congregation that the Lord wants to heal, and invite them up for prayer. The gifts of the Spirit are all supernatural abilities given by the Lord to different members of the Body of Christ as He wills for the purpose of ministry (1 Corinthians 12:11). They are to be used as He initiates. Those who have not experienced seeing these gifts in action may be apprehensive at first, but it should be emphasized that they are given for "the profit of all" (Corinthians 12:7). **They are given to help the Body of Christ.**

Dreams and Visions

But this is what was spoken by the prophet Joel:
'And it shall come to pass in the last days, says God,
That I will pour out My Spirit on all flesh;
Your sons and your daughters shall prophecy,
Your young men shall see visions.
Your old men shall dream dreams.'
Acts 2:16-17

This passage is repeat by Peter on the day of Pentecost of a prophecy given by Joel in the Old Testament (Joel 2:28). It is a prophecy given for those of us who live in the New Testament days—in the last days. We have to be aware that there are three sources of dreams and visions, God, ourselves, and the evil one, so we cannot take every dream or vision as being of God. Most of my dreams are related to what I had to eat before bedtime! But I have had a few dreams in my life that I know were of God, and they have been a blessing in my life. The tests for any dream or vision are: does it line up with the principles of Scripture, and is there a confirming witness of the Holy Spirit.

A vision can be anything from a simple mental impression or image, to something one experiences. Some years ago, as a relatively young believer, my wife and I were at a church picnic on the beach at a seaside town in New Zealand. It was a beautiful day, with blue ocean and sunny skies. One could look out and see Kapiti Island some way out in the ocean. There was nothing out of the ordinary about the day, just a peaceful day by the ocean. Suddenly, the picnic setting was gone, and everything was in black and white, like an old black and white movie. From the coast, all the way out to Kapiti Island, the sea was full of warships. Then the scene changed back to the peaceful seaside church picnic again. I was scared stiff, not having any idea what had happened. I was afraid to tell anyone what I had seen, in case they thought I was losing my mind! It was some time before understanding of what had happened came. There was a lot of spiritual warfare in the area where we were, and the Lord was giving me a picture of that warfare in vision form.

Angelic visits

For there stood by me this night an angel of the God to whom I belong and whom I serve, saying, 'Do not be afraid, Paul; you must be brought before Caesar; and indeed God has granted you all those who sail with you.'
Acts 27:23-24

This is not the usual way God speaks to us, but it happened to some in both Old and New Testament times. God has not changed—He is still the same today—so it can happen in our time too, and especially as we approach the end of the age.

PART 3

GOD HAS MORE FOR YOU

For the path of the just is like the shining sun,
That shines ever brighter unto the perfect day.
Proverbs 4:18

Chapter 15
LIMITED BY A GOLDFISH BOWL

I have come that they may have life, and that they may have it more abundantly.
John 10:10

Jesus came that we may have abundant life. Are we experiencing that abundant life as the norm in our daily lives? Or do we know the words, but not live the experience? For example we could look at a picture of a mouth watering meal and wish we could eat it, or we can sit down at the table and enjoy eating the meal. In Western Christianity we have frequently so majored on having the precisely correct doctrine, and making sure that every "i" is dotted and every "t" crossed, that we have become very short on the joyful experience of living the Christian life, and living it to a full. We have been more like the person admiring the picture of the mouth watering meal than the one sitting down and eating it. While good basic doctrine is essential, that alone cannot fulfill the desire for life that God put on the inside of us, and that Jesus came to make available to us. We were created to enjoy fellowship with our Creator, and to experience the life that only He can give. It is not only eternal life that will never end, but it also a different quality of life—the very life of God Himself—that He wants to share with us. **It is a quality of life that is beyond anything that we can experience without Him.**

One major reason for not experiencing abundant life is failure to abide in Jesus. Another reason for this is our personal "goldfish bowl." What do I mean by a goldfish bowl? It is being confined to a small space in our lives, confined by ungodly boundaries based on our personal limitations. Now God does have boundaries set by His word, but within those boundaries is a much larger area than many of us live in. Some of those ungodly boundaries that confine us are:

What we think and say about ourselves

What others think and say about us

Past mistakes and failures

Being afraid to displease people

Our comfort zones

Having wealth like that rich young ruler, which can hold us back from following Jesus fully

Lack of finances which limits how we think God can use us

Limitations of our education or training

I had my own goldfish bowl, in which I limited what God could do in my life. Several things happened to start the process of coming free, and experiencing more of His abundant life. One day some years ago, the Lord said, "Your thinking is too small for the level you are in." I had been a believer for a number of years, and knew that this was true. I did not even try to argue with or avoid what the Lord had said. I simply agreed with Him and asked Him to change my thinking. The Bible says "For as he thinks in his heart, so is he" (Proverbs 23:7). **How we think has a lot to do with the boundaries of our goldfish bowl.** The process then began. It has been scary at times, for I had to take my eyes off what I could do and my limited resources, and turn my eyes onto the Lord and believe that He would be all I need and provide all I need for what He had in mind for my life. **It was and is an ongoing adventure of faith.**

Really, the Christian life is not as much about who we are, as it is about whom He is, and what He is able to do in and through our lives. **God delights to do extraordinary things through ordinary people. That way, He gets the glory, we get blessed and He uses us to bless others.** If you are an ordinary person you qualify for His extraordinary use! Let us look at several of the Old Testament saints who also struggled with personal goldfish bowls.

Jeremiah

The Bible describes a conversation between the Lord and Jeremiah, part of which is given below.

Then the word of the LORD came to me, saying:

"Before I formed you in the womb I knew you;
Before you were born I sanctified you;
I ordained you a prophet to the nations."
Then said I:
"Ah, Lord God!
Behold I cannot speak, for I am a youth."

But the LORD said to me:

"Do not say, 'I am a youth,'
For you shall go to all to whom I send you,
And whatever I command you, you shall speak.
Do not be afraid of their faces,
For I am with you to deliver you," says the LORD.
Jeremiah 1:4-8

Essentially the Lord was saying "Don't look at yourself and what you think you can or cannot do; I will be with you and that is enough" Later on in verse 9 God says to Jeremiah "Behold I have put My words in your mouth." **What God has for our lives cannot be accomplished on our own. It will take the Presence of God and His enabling for us to carry it out.** If we can do it on our own, we are walking in something far less than He has for us!

Gideon

Another example is that of Gideon, who lived in a time when Israel was being oppressed by a heathen nation, the Midianites (Judges 6: 1-10).

He, along with others, was living in a cave and threshing wheat in a winepress that was hidden from sight, rather than doing it in the open. He was living and working in fear of the Midianites. That was his goldfish bowl. Then one day he had a conversation with the Angel of the Lord. Sometimes the term "Angel of the Lord" is used to describe the Lord Himself; at other times an angelic messenger from God. As you read Judges 6:12-16, it becomes apparent that Gideon is actually speaking with the Lord.

And the Angel of the LORD appeared to him, and said to him, "The Lord is with you, you mighty man of valor!" Gideon said to Him, "O my lord, if the LORD is with us, why then has all this happened to us? And where are all His miracles which our fathers told us about, saying, 'Did not the Lord bring us up from Egypt?' But now the LORD has forsaken us and delivered us into the hands of the Midianites." Then the LORD turned to him and said, "Go in this might of yours, and you shall save Israel from the hand of the Midianites. Have I not sent you?" So he said to Him, "O my Lord, how can I save Israel? Indeed my clan is the weakest in Manasseh, and I am the least in my father's house." And the LORD said to him, "Surely I will be with you, and you shall defeat the Midianites as one man."

Gideon had an encounter that day which challenged his whole way of thinking and was about to take him right out of his goldfish bowl! At the time the Lord spoke to him, Gideon self image was probably rock bottom, and this becomes clear in the conversation. God's picture of Gideon was entirely different. Gideon's picture of himself was based on who he was, not on who God could make him. His response to the Lord's new description of himself was to avoid it by focusing on the predicament that Israel was in, asking why God had forsaken them. The Lord ignores his question, and proceeds to give Gideon his commission to deliver Israel from the Midianites. Gideon again tries to sidestep what God had said by focusing on his complete inadequacy for this commission. He was completely correct in one way. Of himself he was completely inadequate for the task. But God persists by saying "Surely, I will be with you, and you shall defeat the Midianites as one man." God was able to be all that Gideon needed Him to be in carrying out his assignment. Gideon was not naturally a courageous man, but when God called him a mighty man of valor, God was well able to make him one. **The word of God is more than information. It has all the power needed to fulfill it!** Gideon went on to deliver Israel from an entire heathen nation with only 300 men. God gave him every encouragement, and gave him the strategy. God was with him, and that was enough.

We all have reasons that keep us from stepping out in faith when God calls us to go beyond our goldfish bowls. But **God has the power to make you and me whatever He calls us to be**. He is able to enable us in it and to provide all that is needed for it. Our part is very simple. We need to believe what He says about us and to us, and do what He tells us to do, and He will do the rest. It is not complicated, but it will take faith!

CHAPTER 16
GOD HAS MORE FOR YOU

Now to Him who is able to do exceedingly abundantly above all that we ask or think, according to the power that works in us, to Him be glory in the church by Christ Jesus to all generations, forever and ever. Amen

Ephesians 3:20-21

As we saw in the previous chapter, what God has in mind for us is really more about who He is, rather than about who we are. What He has for us to walk in cannot be done in our own strength, own wisdom or own resources. It we limit our thinking to what we can do, or what we can figure out, or to what resources we have, we will never walk in His best for us.

You don't have to feel like an also-ran

An also-ran is someone who runs in a race, but never wins. For many years I considered myself an also-ran. There was no particular reason why I should feel that way, but I did. I had good jobs, but not spectacular ones. I loved teaching Bible and had been able to so from time to time, but in general I felt like Mr. Boringly Average guy. Really, in retrospect, I had no reason to feel that way. I was born and raised in South Africa, had lived and worked in four different countries, and had married a great girl from the USA. Our two children were born in New Zealand, which is a beautiful place and all things considered, my life had been far from boring. But nevertheless the feeling of being an also-ran persisted. Feelings are strange things at times, and do not always respond to logic.

Then, one day through a conversation with a friend, the Lord began to make it clear that He wanted me to write a book on those things that He had been showing me for some years. I had often enjoyed Christian books, and when passing a Christian bookstore I would love to go in and browse, but never considered writing one. There were others who were gifted in that area, and they were the ones to do it. I would just enjoy what they wrote.

I had a choice. My goldfish bowl had the following limits that would have made it impossible for me to write a book. Firstly, I had no formal training in writing. I was a Physics major who had worked in or taught Electronics and associated subjects most of my life. Secondly, I had no idea as to how to go about getting a book published. Absolutely none! Thirdly, I had no money available for its publication as we lived from paycheck to paycheck. I had a choice to make. I could allow the limitations of my gold fish bowl to prevent me working on a book, or I could believe God and start work!

Faith requires that we act without seeing in advance how it's all going to work out. It is like walking towards a closed door, believing it will open when we get there. If we wait to see the door open before we act, that is not faith, but sight, and if we limit ourselves to only doing what we can see or figure out in advance, we are not living by faith. I was being asked to do something I had never done before and was not trained to do. In addition, I had to believe that it would get published even though I had no idea how, and to believe that the money needed would become available when it was needed, even though I did not have it now. The project was rather a daunting one to say the least.

With some trepidation I began to write. I had to fit it in with the requirements of home life and job, and there were delays that I had no control over. There were times when working on it came easily and other times I would get stuck on a section and would have to work it and keep reworking it until I was happy with that section. Through it all I experienced the Lord helping me step by step. It was hard work at times and fun at other times, but I found myself enjoying this new experience and feeling fulfilled doing it. Two years after starting, by the grace of God, *Standing Firm in a Time of Shaking* was published.

Then something rather remarkable happened. In stepping outside my goldfish bowl, and doing something that was well outside the boundaries of it, I no longer felt like an also-ran! I have come to realize that when we live within the confines of our gold fish bowls, we often feel like also-rans. It is because God has more for us to walk in. It is not that we are in competition with others, nor is it that we should compare ourselves with others. Each one of us is unique, and God has a unique plan for each of our lives. From His perspective, each plan is of great value, and God loves each of us equally. I believe that once we are born again believers, we sense on the inside of us that God has a purpose for us to walk in. When we are walking in less than He has for us, or on the wrong track for our lives, we feel unfulfilled and like also-rans.

When we step outside the limitations of our goldfish bowls, or the put it another way, get out of the boat and start to walk by faith in obedience to our Heavenly Father, we experience living like His children. When we do this, there is a fulfillment that comes from living the way we were designed to live as His sons and daughters. **Inside the boat we can experience a taste of His life. But it is only when we get out of the boat, and live in faith and obedience beyond its limitations, that we begin to experience the abundant life that Jesus came to give us!**

CHAPTER 17
THE POWER TO WALK IN YOUR CALLING

For we are His workmanship, created in Christ Jesus for good works, which God prepared beforehand that we should walk in them.
Ephesians 2:10

Each born again believer has a calling, and in that calling God has good works for us to accomplish by His grace, that He prepared for us to walk in beforehand. Generally, we do not know what that calling is when we are born again. We are spiritually babes in Christ. However, as we grow that calling is progressively revealed to us. For some it may come all at once in a moment of inspiration; for others it may be a growing awareness that takes place over a period of time. But however it comes, the Lord will continually take us into more if we are willing. As we go on in our journey with Him, we will continue to grow and expand and receive further revelation of that calling.

Now God has created good works in advance—works of obedience in His service—for each of us to walk in. He designed each of us uniquely to walk in those works. When there is a match, i.e. when we walk in that which we were created for, there is a wonderful fulfillment that takes place. No amount of money, position or status can compare with the inner peace, joy and fulfillment of walking with Him in what we were created for.

A word of caution is needed here. Relationship with the Lord must come before works. This takes us back to the First Priority. The writer of Ecclesiastes accomplished many great works, but found that these great works by themselves left him feeling that life was vain and empty of meaning. God created us for relationship with Himself, and **when we walk with Him** in that which He has created us to do, we experience life and life more abundantly!

The Power for Service—The Baptism in the Holy Spirit

I indeed baptized you with water, but He will baptize you with the Holy Spirit. Mark 1:8

These words were spoken by John the Baptist concerning Jesus. What is the baptism in the Holy Spirit? Let me say upfront that what we will be talking about here is not the salvation experience, but power for service. A person who has received Jesus as Savior and Lord, and has a real relationship with Him, is saved. When a person is born again, The Holy Spirit comes and lives in him or her, and that person has become a child of God!

Before Jesus left his disciples and ascended He said "Behold, I send the Promise of My Father upon you; but tarry in the city of Jerusalem until you are endued with power from on high" (Luke 24:49). He also said "But you shall receive power when the Holy Spirit has come upon you; and you shall be witnesses to Me in Jerusalem, and in all Judea and Samaria, and to the end of the earth" (Acts 1:8). The commission that Jesus gave His disciples was to be carried out in the power of the Holy Spirit. They were to wait for that power to come upon them before proceeding with that commission. When Jesus spoke these words, He was not talking to the disciples about their salvation, but about the power they would need for service.

The Holy Spirit is the One who gives us the power to do what God has designed us for. He is the Helper, the Comforter, and the Strengthener. He is the One who leads us into all truth. He is the Author of the Bible, inspiring men as they wrote it. He is the One who gives us spiritual understanding and revelation of what the Scriptures mean. He is with us and in us. God did not leave us to run this Christian race on our own!

How do you know whether or not you have received that power for service in your life? I had been saved for many years and really did not know whether there was more of God available for me. I knew I needed more, but was unable to find out how to get more. Then I met people who talked about the baptism in the Holy Spirit. I really did not understand what this was all about, so one day I simply asked the Lord to give me more, if there was more. Wonderfully, He gave me more! Happily, God looks at the desire and cry of our hearts, and does not go by how much or little we understand. Understanding for me came after the experience. **If we are truly hungry for more of God, He will meet us where we are at.**

Now we all come from different backgrounds, and may use different terminology for the experience of the empowering of the Holy Spirit for service. The Baptism in the Spirit, the release of the Spirit, or simply being filled with the Spirit, are some of the ways this experience is described. If we feel that we need more of God in our lives, we should simply and humbly ask Him for it. The important thing is our hunger level for more of God. He does not respond to superficial requests, **but when we really, really want more of Him, He will surely answer. He wants to give us more of Himself!** Jesus said "Blessed are those who hunger and thirst for righteousness, for they shall be filled" (Matthew 5:6).

Continually Filled with the Spirit
And do not be drunk with wine, in which is dissipation; but be filled with the Spirit
Ephesians 5:18

The command given in this verse is not just for some special believers, but for every believer. The meaning of this verse is to **continually** be filled with the Spirit. In other words, once we have been filled with the Spirit, we need to stay filled! Consider the experience of the early church.

On the day of Pentecost the disciples were filled with the Spirit. The sound of a rushing mighty wind where they met, and tongues of fire appearing and sitting on each of their heads, accompanied that experience. God showed up in an incredible and powerful way (Acts 2:1-4). They received a new power and boldness in their lives. They were also supernaturally able to speak in the tongues of other nationalities so that the Gospel message could be understood by all present. One would think that after a powerful experience like that, they would surely not need to be filled with the Spirit again! However, let us look at an account in Acts where Peter and John were arrested for preaching, and brought before the religious authorities. They were forbidden to speak or teach in the name of Jesus. They refused, choosing to please God rather than man, and after being further threatened they were released and went back to their fellow believers. During their prayer time together, something rather amazing happened as described in Acts 4:29-31.

"Now, Lord, look on their threats, and grant to Your servants that with all boldness they may speak Your word, by stretching out Your hand to heal, and that signs and wonders may be done through the name of Your holy Servant Jesus." And when they had prayed, the place where they were assembled together was shaken; and they were all filled with the Holy Spirit, and they spoke the word of God with boldness.

If they needed to be filled again with the Holy Spirit, so do we. The Holy Spirit was sent to us when Jesus left, to enable us to live the Christian life in fullness. We are designed to live as Spirit filled believers. This requires that we not only be filled with the Spirit once, wonderful as that is, but that we stay filled with the Spirit on an ongoing basis. He is God in us and with us. God gives us His Spirit and His Word, to lead and empower us to live the Christian life, and to fulfill our callings. He has not left us on our own to muddle through somehow!

Many of us, and I include myself, have spent much of our Christian lives running on half full or empty. We are designed to live lives that are full to overflowing with the Holy Spirit, and to serve and minster out of that fullness. Romans 12:11 says "Never lag in zeal *and* in earnest endeavor; be aglow *and* burning with the Spirit, serving the Lord" (AMP). We are not called to burn out for Jesus, but to burn brightly for Him. We are not called to live the Christian life by our own efforts and wisdom but in His. **We can only truly fulfill our callings in His sufficiency.**

How to stay filled with the Spirit

He who believes in Me, as the Scripture has said, out of his heart will flow rivers of living water.

John 7:38

The Holy Spirit lives in each of us who are believers, and because of that there is a well of living water inside our innermost beings. When that well is flowing, living water flows out of us, **rivers of living water.**

In the natural, if we have a well in the yard, we want to be able to get water from that well whenever we need it. Sometimes the pump gets dry, and won't pump water, so that even though there is water in the well, we cannot access it. If we pour a little water into the pump—prime the pump—the water will start to flow again.

Spiritually, we can run dry and not know how to get the well of living water flowing again on the inside of us. We just know that we are dry, and God seems far away. Below are given some Biblical ways to "prime the pump" and keep the river of the Spirit flowing in our lives. I don't claim that this is a complete list, but it is what I have come to know so far. With the exception of the first way (the First Priority), there is no particular priority order given. We are all different and the priority order may be different for each of us.

• **Abiding in Jesus and letting His words abide—live—in us** (John 15). Our relationship with the Lord and His Word are of paramount importance. This remains the First Priority.

• **Wholehearted and exuberant praise and worship** (Psalm 148, 149, 150). This includes singing, raising our hands, for some using musical instruments, for some dancing, and generally everyone entering in wholeheartedly! Many, who have no difficulty being enthusiastic and demonstrative in their support for their sports team, freeze up and have great difficulty being exuberant in a church service. These Psalms and other passages make it clear that God wants us to be even more enthusiastic about Him than about our favorite sports team! There is a real release and an anointing that takes place in an atmosphere of wholehearted praise and worship. It is almost impossible to depressed, defeated, or discouraged in that kind of atmosphere.

- **Giving thanks, and having an attitude of gratitude** (Psalm 100:4, 1 Thessalonians 5:18). In the world, complaining and griping when things don't go our way is the norm. I used to love griping and complaining and finding a bunch of people that I could do this with. However, nothing ever improved in the situation I griped about by doing this. Nothing! As a Christian the Lord made it clear that He was not pleased with my attitude, and He worked in my heart to change me. We looked at the benefits of thankfulness in a previous chapter. It is a much happier way to live and it allows God to make whatever situation we find ourselves in work for our good. Thankfulness also helps release the flow of the life of God within us in the midst of the situation.

- **Prayer** (Philippians 4:6-7). Prayer keeps us in two-way communication with Him, who is the Source of our life. It allows us to cast all our cares, worries and anxieties upon Him, be strengthened in our faith and receive more of His peace. If you are also able to pray in tongues, it is a wonderful way to build yourself up in your faith as well as priming the pump (Jude 20, 1 Corinthians 14:15).

- **Fellowship with other wholehearted believers** (Matthew 18:20, Hebrews 10:24-25). When a hot coal is taken out of the fire and left in its own for too long, it cools down and turns grey. When it is with other hot coals it keeps glowing with red heat. When we become joined in fellowship with other alive, on fire believers, it helps us to stay on fire ourselves, and our being with others helps them too. There are times when we are unavoidably unable to have regular fellowship, and the Lord's grace will sustain us in those times. But when isolation and sporadic fellowship becomes the norm, we are in trouble!

- **Using the gifts God has given us**.

Therefore I remind you to stir up the gift of God which is in you through the laying on of my hands. For God has not given us a spirit of fear, but of power and of love and of a sound mind.

2 Timothy 1:6-7

We are reminded to stir up the gifts God has imparted to us. We often wait until we feel like it, or feel spiritual before using the gifts we have been given. When we step out in faith and start to use these gifts, we "prime the pump" and life starts to flow through us. Certainly we should wait for God to initiate, **but I believe that many times God simply wants us to get moving in what He has given us, and is waiting for us to start!** As we start moving, He will direct us.

Chapter 18
KINGDOM MINISTRY

Kingdom ministry involves several things. Firstly there is the preaching of the Gospel message. Secondly this is to be accompanied by demonstrations of kingdom power—healing, deliverance, signs and wonders that confirm the message. Thirdly, there should also be the making of disciples accompanied by changed lives. The growth of Christ-centered recovery ministries is an encouraging example of this.

However, in the West many churches have largely avoided the second area—the supernatural manifestation of the power of God in healing, deliverance and the miraculous. I believe that this is in the process of changing. The Lord is restoring the church to kingdom power; anything less in the days we are living in will not work, or will be far less effective than is needed in this challenging time. The world around us is not impressed by words alone; they need to see tangible evidence of kingdom power to back up our words. Increasing numbers are turning to the wrong kind of supernatural, ranging from the bogus, to supernatural manifestations of the evil one. The world needs to see the real thing, for our God is so much greater! If we are to present a true and complete Gospel message, then we need to know how Jesus did it, and how the early church did it. Then we will be able to follow their examples and apply them to the way we present the Gospel in our day.

How Jesus Ministered

And Jesus went about all Galilee, teaching in their synagogues, preaching the gospel of the kingdom, and healing all kinds of sickness and all kinds of disease among the people.

Matthew 4:23

Men of Israel, hear these words: Jesus of Nazareth, a Man attested by God to you by miracles, wonders, and signs which God did through Him in your midst, as you yourselves also know—

Acts 2:22

Then Jesus went about all the cities and villages, teaching in their synagogues, preaching the gospel of the kingdom, and healing every sickness and every disease among the people.

Matthew 9:35

It is clear from these passages that when Jesus taught, kingdom power was manifested. There was no separation between the preaching of the Word and the power of the kingdom. God backs up His Word with His power, and in the life and ministry of Jesus, this is clearly demonstrated. Jesus healed the sick, delivered people from demonic oppression, miraculously fed multitudes, turned water into wine, walked on water and raised the dead. He demonstrated that the power of His kingdom was greater than the natural power of man, and greater than the power of the evil one. **Jesus is indeed Lord of all!**

How the Early Church Ministered

The early church was commissioned, as we still are, to be actively involved in the Great Commission. He delegated to His followers the authority to carry this out in His Name.

And Jesus came and spoke to them, saying, "All authority has been given to Me in heaven and on earth. Go therefore and make disciples of all the nations, baptizing them in the name of the Father and of the Son and of the Holy Spirit, teaching them to observe all things that I have commanded you; and lo, I am with you always, *even* to the end of the age." Amen.

Matthew 28:18-20

The way they did this is illustrated in the following passages:

And they went out and preached everywhere, the Lord working with *them* and confirming the word through the accompanying signs. Amen.

Mark 16:20

And with many other words he testified and exhorted them, saying, "Be saved from this perverse generation." Then those who gladly received his word were baptized; and that day about three thousand souls were added *to them*. And they continued steadfastly in the apostles' doctrine and fellowship, in the breaking of bread, and in prayers. Then fear came upon every soul, and many wonders and signs were done through the apostles.

Acts 2:40-43

And through the hands of the apostles many signs and wonders were done among the people. And they were all with one accord in Solomon's Porch.

Acts 5:12

Therefore they stayed there a long time, speaking boldly in the Lord, who was bearing witness to the word of His grace, granting signs and wonders to be done by their hands.

Acts 14:3

It is clear from these and other Scriptures that the early church ministered the way that Jesus had done before He ascended. The Gospel message that they preached and taught was accompanied by signs, wonders and miracles that powerfully confirmed the authenticity of their message.

How Should We Minister?

If Jesus preached and taught with manifestations of kingdom power confirming what He said, and if the early church followed His example, then it clear that this is the way that we should minster too. In fairness there is a part of the Body of Christ in this nation that is walking in this kind of ministry, but it is a minority.

Why is this so? Some reasons are listed below. There may be others, but these are some obvious ones.

- **Wrong teaching**—many believers have been taught that the gifts of the Spirit, and signs, wonders and miracles are not for today. If a person believes this, they are unable to have faith that the Lord still moves through His Body in the same way today. God does not change, His ways do not change, and "Jesus Christ *is* the same yesterday, today, and forever" (Hebrews 13:8).

- **Our comfort zones**—comfortable Christianity that we can control is not threatening to us or others. If we really let God be in charge of our lives and of our meetings, then He may move in ways that we are not used to, even though they are Biblical. He will be in control not us. That is always a wonderful thing, but it is not always a comfortable thing! It we love comfort more than growth, we will not want to move out of where we are comfortable into more of what God has for us.

- **The fear of man**—this is something that keeps many from experiencing more of God. If we are more concerned about looking good to others and pleasing them, than about pleasing God, we will not do anything that might make us seem foolish or displease others. I found out painfully some years ago that I could not consistently please God and man at the same time. Paul said, "For do I now persuade men, or God? Or do I seek to please men? For if I still pleased men, I would not be a bondservant of Christ" (Gal 1:10).

- **Many believers** are unfamiliar with preaching and teaching with signs following. It is difficult for believers who have never seen or experienced the miraculous to believe beyond their experience. This is very understandable reason. We are very blessed to live in a country where so much is provided for us. Most of us have a place to live, enjoy very regular meals, have all the modern conveniences. Most of us have not only what we need, but way beyond that! However, in this environment it is hard for our faith to grow strong. In much of the world, people have a lot less, and believers need to pray regularly for daily needs that we take for granted. As they experience God meeting their needs, their faith grows through regular daily use. When something big comes along, they are more able to have faith to believe God to come through for them. Most of us are not prepared to deal with big things because our faith has not had daily training in smaller things. The faith of many of us has become weak and out of shape from lack of regular use. One of the plus sides of the tough economic season that we have entered, is our faith is going to have to grow! We will no longer be able to take for granted that everything that we need will be provided for us by man. We are going to increasingly need to look to the Lord to provide for those needs in natural and supernatural ways. **We will need to live by His promises. God is a big God and a wonderful Father. He is well able to take care of us in these tough times!**

Experiencing the God of the Miraculous

As has been said, many believers have not experienced God moving miraculously in their lives. Of course, salvation is a totally supernatural and miraculous experience! One is not born again naturally, but supernaturally. In my life, I was introduced to the miraculous in an unexpected way. My wife and I left Canada and went out to New Zealand in 1971. The New Zealand Government offered to pay our way out if I would work for them for at least three years, and I was a needy graduate student looking for a job. Getting the job was in fact a miracle in itself. It turned out that the person in New Zealand advertising the job had been in the same carpool as my college supervisor during the Second World War. They had both worked for the Royal Radar establishment in Britain during that war, and knew each other. That gave me an advantage that no other applicant had! As a result I got a job working for the Department of Scientific and Industrial Research.

During that time I met a fellow Christian at work, who invited my wife and me to an interdenominational meeting shortly before Christmas of our first year in New Zealand. He drove us into the capital city, Wellington, to an Anglican (Episcopalian in the USA) cathedral. It was unlike any church meeting that we had ever been to. It was a mixture of all ages and varieties of people. There were young people dressed casually, some Catholic nuns, Maori Pentecostals, people in suits and just an amazing mixture. The singing was lively—in fact the whole service was lively. At the end of the meeting, it was announced that anyone wanting prayer for healing could come to one side and be prayed for. I had a chronic acid reflux condition that had troubled me for about seven years.

I had been told by a specialist that I probably had a hiatus hernia—a condition where the membrane in the esophagus is torn, allowing acid from the stomach to get back into the esophagus and damage it. I had to sleep on a bed with bricks under one end to elevate the head, so that acid would not run back into my esophagus at night. I had almost continuous heart burn, and it was so bad I would drink antacid out of the bottle without measuring it. I could not drink orange juice or anything that would irritate that area more. It was bad. Here I was in a new country, virtually unknown. It is sometimes easier to be adventurous in a place where one is unknown than in one's home town! What did I have to lose?

I went up to the side of the church and asked for prayer for healing from this condition. I man put his hand on me and prayed for me in the name of Jesus. I felt nothing and went back to my seat, and shortly after that we got back into the car, and the friend drove us home. The trip was 20 to 30 minutes long, and as we drove the pain in my esophagus began to ease. By the time we got home it was completely gone! To cut a long story short, we got rid of the bricks under the bed, I no longer needed antacid or pills to stop acid reflux, and I could drink orange juice and eat anything I liked. I was healed. Over 30 years later, I am still healed! I had previously met Jesus as my Savior and Lord. Now I met Him as my Healer. God is an awesome God. Over the years, I have had the privilege of seeing God move in miraculous ways. I believe that we are living in a season where God is revealing Himself in wonderful ways. **He does not require us to be ahead of where we are at, but if we will regularly use the faith we have, and be open to the fact that God is much bigger than we thought He was, our faith and experience of Him will grow. He will take us from faith to faith!**

For I am not ashamed of the gospel of Christ, for it is the power of God to salvation for everyone who believes, for the Jew first and also for the Greek. For in it the righteousness of God is revealed from faith to faith; as it is written, *"The just shall live by faith."*
Romans 1:16-17

CHAPTER 19
THE PATH OF LIGHT IS GETTING BRIGHTER

But the path of the just is like the shining sun,
That shines ever brighter unto the perfect day.
The way of the wicked is like darkness;
They do not know what makes them stumble.
Proverbs 4:18-19

As we approach the end of the age, there is an increase taking place of both light and darkness. For those who are walking in the light that they have, and who are actively following Jesus, the light is increasing. More truth, more of God's glory, more revelation of the Word of God, and more of God's Presence are being experienced. For those outside Christ, travelling on the path of their own way, the gloom is gathering. Society around us is stumbling around in deepening darkness, not knowing where it is going.

Believers who are camping in their comfort zones are in a precarious position. There is no such thing as being able to drift in the Christian life. Those who drift will invariably drift away from Christ. If they continue to ignore the promptings of the Lord to rise up and follow Him, they will lose even the light that they have, and find themselves falling back into confusion and darkness. This is no time to be a lukewarm, semi-committed believer!

Another thing that is happening as we approach the end of this age is that evidences of both the kingdom of Heaven and the kingdom of the evil one are increasing in the world. Manifestations of the kingdom of God—healings, signs wonders and miracles—are increasing and will continue to increase as the end of this age approaches. Manifestations of the evil kingdom, such as the rise in terrorism, the growing interest in the occult, and the general rise of lawlessness worldwide are also taking place.

It is the best of times, or the worst of times, depending on whether one is walking on the path of the righteous in increasing light, or the path leading away from Christ and of deepening darkness. For many years in Western and affluent nations, there has not been much difference in lifestyle between many believers and many unbelievers. This has not been the case in nations where it can be costly to be a believer. However, in the West the grey shades of sitting on the fence are fast disappearing. We have come to a fork in the road, and if we have not chosen yet, we will be forced to choose between the path of light and life, or the path of darkness and destruction. Our loyalty to Christ must come before every other earthly loyalty if we are to stay on the path of light and life. Compromise will rapidly become a thing of the past, as those who have been sitting the fence choose to wholeheartedly follow Jesus, or wholeheartedly go the way of the world.

For you who have already decided to follow Jesus, a glorious adventure of faith lies ahead in the fellowship of the Master and in His service. It will not be without cost, but it will be glorious. Whatever happens, don't quit! Take a break to recover from the battle when needed, but don't quit. God loves you and has a glorious future for you, more wonderful than anything you can imagine!

Therefore we do not lose heart. Even though our outward man is perishing, yet the inward *man* is being renewed day by day. For our light affliction, which is but for a moment, is working for us a far more exceeding *and* eternal weight of glory, while we do not look at

the things which are seen, but at the things which are not seen. For the things which are seen *are* temporary, but the things which are not seen *are* eternal.

2 Corinthians 4:16-18

Contact Information

Dan de Kock may be contacted via email at
growinfaith@comcast.net
Website address www.growinginfaith.vpweb.com